Focus on Thinking

# Focus on Thinking

*Engaging Students in Higher-Order Thinking*

Paul A. Wagner, Daphne D. Johnson, Frank Fair, and Daniel Fasko Jr.

ROWMAN & LITTLEFIELD
Lanham • Boulder • New York • London

Published by Rowman & Littlefield
A wholly owned subsidiary of The Rowman & Littlefield Publishing Group, Inc.
4501 Forbes Boulevard, Suite 200, Lanham, Maryland 20706
www.rowman.com

Unit A, Whitacre Mews, 26-34 Stannary Street, London SE11 4AB

Copyright © 2017 by Paul A. Wagner, Daphne D. Johnson, Frank Fair, and Daniel Fasko Jr.

*All rights reserved.* No part of this book may be reproduced in any form or by any electronic or mechanical means, including information storage and retrieval systems, without written permission from the publisher, except by a reviewer who may quote passages in a review.

British Library Cataloguing in Publication Information Available

**Library of Congress Cataloging-in-Publication Data Available**

ISBN 978-1-4758-3351-5 (cloth : alk. paper)
ISBN 978-1-4758-3352-2 (pbk. : alk. paper)
ISBN 978-1-4758-3353-9 (electronic)

∞ ™ The paper used in this publication meets the minimum requirements of American National Standard for Information Sciences Permanence of Paper for Printed Library Materials, ANSI/NISO Z39.48-1992.

Printed in the United States of America

*This book is dedicated to several important people in our lives:*

*Paul A. Wagner dedicates this book to his youngest daughter Emily. He hopes that she will enjoy a lifetime at the crossroads of the disciplines and always enjoy an occasion to participate in The Great Conversation of Humankind.*

*Daphne D. Johnson dedicates this book to all the teachers who have touched her life—from her first grade teacher, Mrs. Babik to her Dissertation Chair, Dr. Robert Williams. All have had an impact.*

*Frank Fair dedicates this book to Dick Cording. He is grateful to Dick because Dick was kind enough to hire him to teach philosophy and to provide an inspiring example to follow.*

*Daniel Fasko Jr. dedicates this book in the memory of his parents, Barbara and Daniel Fasko, who instilled in him the desire to think critically and to contribute to our society.*

# Contents

| | |
|---|---|
| Preface | ix |
| Acknowledgments | xi |
| Introduction | xiii |
| 1  A Focus on Thinking | 1 |
| 2  Middle School Scripts | 13 |
| 3  Secondary School Scripts | 39 |
| Appendix A: Resources for Further Information | 71 |
| Appendix B: Building Your Own Scripts | 77 |
| Appendix C: Elements of Mindware | 89 |
| References | 99 |
| Author Index | 103 |
| Subject Index | 107 |
| About the Authors | 111 |

# Preface

We are four academics whose experiences cut across the arts and sciences and education, and as well we have firsthand experience with eight different states' public education systems. Each of us from our own perspective has seen junior high school and secondary students struggle to increase the efficiency with which they retrieve information for high-stakes standardized testing. At the same time they struggle with information recall, it seems they find less and less opportunity to engage in the cooperative and collaborative skill sets required for figuring things out alone or collectively in a group of inspired and inspiring thinkers.

The need for developing critical-creative thinking stirred each of us into our own efforts to develop these skills in firsthand engagement with students. In addition, our individual research efforts and consulting activities put each of us into close proximity with the challenges we address in this book to amplify students' intellectual horizons by giving them a chance to engage in something we call the Great Conversation of Humankind.

The teachers we have worked with over the years are grieved that they have more and more tasks imposed upon them and less opportunity for either teacher training in critical thinking or teaching critical thinking to students. Herein we have set out scripts, strategies, and descriptions of elements of critical thinking that can be used at the spur of the moment by any teacher willing to take on the challenge.

Our foremost desire is that, at the end of increasingly many days, teachers can feel satisfied that they have sent their students home thinking, pondering, and likely to continue their pensive speculations with others at home. Good discussions never quite die out. Education should never feel over to students just because they have left the building for the day.

# Acknowledgments

This has been a team effort, and each member is responsible for every well-honed instruction as each of us is responsible for whatever faults remain. We represent a swath of academic disciplines relevant to critical thinking, and that swath is ever wider as we reflect on others who helped along our individual thinking over the years.

**Paul A. Wagner** owes much to Matt Lipman, who more or less took me under his wing long ago when I was a graduate student in the 1970s. But equally I owe a debt to Israel Scheffler, who did the same without any expectation of discipleship in return. Chris Lucas tolerated my obsession with philosophy, allowing that I may find a way for it to improve pedagogical practice while I freelanced at the University of Missouri Laboratory School.

During a year at Harvard long ago, Hillary Putnam was kind enough to let me sit in on his class and over lunch and at receptions broaden my appreciation for a philosopher who cares more about getting things right rather than insisting he is right. Finally, Pat Suppes put me up at the Institute for the Mathematical Study of the Social Sciences at Stanford. From Pat I learned to stand in awe of a mind with laserlike focus. Pat could spot an explanatory flaw in an instant. Yet he was always kind, disposing of it without inhibiting further intellectual adventures by those less able.

**Daphne D. Johnson** is forever indebted to her parents, McNeil and Sara Johnson. Their love, support, high expectations, and continued encouragement created an environment for all of their children to be successful.

**Frank Fair** would like to gratefully acknowledge the influence of several people on his involvement in philosophy at various points from high school to PhD work: Joseph John Sikora, Thomas Magner, Edward MacKinnon, Tony Nemetz, and Bowman Clarke.

**Daniel Fasko Jr.** first and foremost thanks his wife, Sharla, for her continued patience and support with my writing endeavors. I truly appreciate her critical comments and suggestions to help me be a more proficient and effective writer.

We would also like to thank Thomas Koerner, Will True, and Carlie Wall of Rowman & Littlefield for their encouragement, thoughtful comments, and assistance with this book.

# Introduction

Country and Western singer Roger Miller once sang, "Everything changes a little as it should, 'cause good ain't forever and bad ain't for good." This clever and hopeful line echoes what Heraclitus opined more than two millennia ago when he said you can never put your foot in the same stream; the water flows endlessly and so all is changing. Writers in India and China and probably in most other cultures have echoed these same metaphysical suspicions. Today this theme of an ever-changing universe has become the mantra of those who deny any access to even plausible truth and insist all is forever relative.

Philosophers, sociologists, and scientists of every type have grappled with this possibility. Thomas Kuhn, the only author who had a book cited more often in a decade than the Bible in more than a hundred years, became famous for the idea of paradigm shifts. In his *The Structure of Scientific Revolutions* he explains, in sympathy with philosopher and aeronautical engineer Norwood Hanson (1958), that all scientific observations are unavoidably contaminated by the theoretical concepts of a dominating research paradigm (Kuhn, 1970, p. 113). In short, there are no theory-free observations. But what does this actually mean?

Are we to believe there is no way to know the world? Is there no truth of the matter? Are all knowledge claims nothing more than favored linguistic commitments of a culture? Are there no ideas better than others? What are we to make of all of this? Is the search for knowledge destined forever to be fruitless? Does thinking private and collectively aim at anything other than agreement on social conventions?

Help in answering all of these questions comes from Thomas Kuhn himself. One of the coauthors of this book, Paul Wagner, had written a piece on Kuhn's message for education many years ago (Wagner, 1983). In 1985,

Wagner and Kuhn had lunch near the MIT campus and talked about what Kuhn saw as a general misunderstanding of his work. Wagner had a copy of Kuhn's latest book at the time, titled *Black-Body Theory and the Quantum Discontinuity, 1894–1912* (1987). Kuhn offered to write a note in Wagner's copy of the book and then explained its importance. Kuhn wrote, "This is my best book."

Kuhn explained that *Structure* has led to much misunderstanding. Kuhn said not only is he not an epistemic relativist, but as a physicist he counts himself as a scientific realist. He said he would like the interested public to know where he truly stands. He elaborated saying that there is a world "out there." We can make judgments about the world that may be right, approximately right, wrong, or not even wrong. Our reasoning is not recklessly impaled upon mere suspicion or conceptual imprisonment imposed by cultural tradition.

Our observations about the world are tainted by our theoretical constructs whether professionally or culturally imposed. But through reasoning and testing ideas against nature humans find their way further from previous error. Reasoning practices, such as avoiding contradiction, the difference between implication and inference, the law of noncontradiction, and so on, give us self-correcting mechanisms to our more transient theoretically based observations. So what are we to learn from this with regard to education and, more specifically, for using the contents of this book?

Much of what we teach in the various school disciplines is formatted for students to recognize answers on standardized objective tests. This does not teach anyone how to reason a path further away from current conventionally held errors. As Nobel Laureate Richard Feynman opined (as cited in Feynman & Leighton, 1985, p. 303), "The path to the Nobel Prize begins with a question." In this book and, in the full *spirit* of STEM education generally, we show teachers how to promote sustained attention to a line of questioning as opposed to a mere solicitation of diverse opinions. In addition, we show how the systematic reasoning Kuhn advocates can be acquired and employed to move inquiry forward to an ever-greater approximation of reality.

The world is waiting to be explored. There will be theories and observations that pave the way to greater understanding. But it is reasoning, and ever-better well-reasoned experimentation, that leads to better schemata for understanding than those employed in the past. Attention to reasoning is what illustrates the decay of a failing paradigm, and it is attention to reasoning that illuminates new conceptualizations. Core curricula and standardized testing are not suited to developing skills of reasoning. In this volume there are whole chapters of scripted discussions that afford teachers a chance to maximize the development of reasoning in the ever-fleeting teachable moment.

Following the first chapter, which further explains the rationale behind a focus on the teaching of reasoning, there are two chapters of scripts for middle school and secondary school students. These scripts cover everything from morals to evidence probability, evolution, and chance, to name just a few topics. The book concludes with three appendices that should serve as resources for the teacher for a long time to come.

Appendix A describes a number of resources for the teacher from critical-thinking centers around the world. The appendix also gives information on a website the authors will maintain to answer reader questions and direct readers to even further resources beyond those mentioned in the appendix.

Appendix B is an excerpt from an earlier book of ours that describes how an enterprising teacher might venture into preparing scripted discussions on his or her own. Appendix C is a sketch of logic because the typical middle and secondary school teacher may have had no training in formal thinking practices, and these benchmarks of good thinking strategies and red flags alerting fallacious reasoning may prove invaluable to the teacher in numerous ways well beyond the immediate employment of scripted discussions.

Critical thinking is not something one acquires simply by declaring oneself a good thinker. Most people declare themselves to be good thinkers just as most declare themselves to be more moral than others (Ariely, 2012; Bazerman & Tenbrunsel, 2011).

The fact is, however, that Aristotle was right when he explained that you become just by doing just acts, temperate by doing temperate acts, and so on. A person becomes a better thinker by engaging in well-crafted discussions that neither meander nor dictate truth. Discussions that lead away from systematic error are rigorous and call for great truth-seeking authenticity by all participants. The scripted exercises in this book make better thinkers by engaging students and teachers in better thinking practices.

*Chapter One*

# A Focus on Thinking

Frans de Waal tells us that Charles Darwin believed animals think and have all sorts of emotional experiences. In sympathy with Darwin, de Waal explains further that the *capacity* to think one's way through the challenges of one's immediate environment is an essential evolutionary trait (de Waal, 2016). The capacity to think using a variety of richly textured languages made humans, in the words of mathematical biologist Martin Nowak (2012), the "supercooperators" and hence masters of our universe. And we can learn to think even better.

Humans are weak, slow, and not especially gifted in other resources of the senses. Indeed, more than once in our evolutionary history our ancestors almost became extinct (Mlodinow, 2016). Somehow we developed tools of thought that far exceeded those of all other animals and even our closest primate cousins (Taylor, 2010). The most important of those tools are the languages that made our native tongues possible, mathematical language possible, and even efficient computer languages possible.

Our languages and instinct for cooperation made possible the invention of the promise (Axelrod & Hamilton, 1981). Through promising we amplify our ability to cooperate with one another across generations and geographic borders. Mathematics and derived computer languages extend our capacity to speculate. Before such languages existed we could only wonder in befuddlement at all that is around us (Tomasello, 2014). Languages brought us into what we call the Great Conversation of Humankind.

Human thinking extends far beyond the immediate demands of survival (Bowles & Gintis, 2011; Wainer, 2016). Our thoughts in the form of enriched linguistic and mathematical expression give rise to intellectual powers for understanding and even reshaping our world (Moore, 2004). The powers of human thinking are greatly amplified through shared communication comprising philosophy, the arts, and the sciences (Tomasello, 2014).

Philosophers were the first to "look in the mirror" and reflect systematically on how thinking can be improved. Aristotle, for example, created a square of opposition to illustrate how arguments can make sound claims as well as go awry. Critical thinking has ever since been the heart and soul of philosophy. In the past two centuries other scholars from fields such as applied mathematics, biology, and the social sciences have joined in the search for optimal skills and dispositions in reasoning.

In the nineteenth century, the mathematician George Boole imagined that all thinking was symbol manipulation. At about the same time, Swiss crystallographer Louis Albert Necker studied human perception experimentally. Experiment and rigorous formal modeling have shaped the study of human mental life and its improvement ever since.

Developmental and cognitive psychologists such as Piaget, Kohlberg, Miller, Bloom, and Bruner tried early on in the mid-twentieth century to show how thinking skills naturally unfold developmentally and how those same skills can be improved. Developmentalists and cognitivists also identified limitations in thinking potency and common distractions impeding thinking excellence. In particular, George Miller (1956) showed symbol manipulation was limited to chunks not exceeding nine bits of information.

Noble Laureate Herbert Simon (1984) later stressed that human rationality was bounded. He constructed computer software to model human mental life and show what humans can and cannot do intellectually. Since Simon's work, a number of Nobel Laureates in economics such as Gary Becker, John Nash, and most recently Daniel Kahneman, have turned much of the social sciences on their heads by showing that humans are not simply rational and self-interested. Humans are robustly thoughtful and compassionate too (Wagner, 2013).

Economists and psychologists developed game scenarios such as the Ultimatum Game and the Dictator Game to study human variants to self-interest and rational inference (Gneezy & Rustichini, 2000). Humans around the world will accept costs to themselves at times in order to punish a stranger who is greedy (Herrmann, Thoni, & Gachter, 2008). That seems neither rational nor self-interested.

But research has shown it is clearly a part of the human picture (Fehr & Fischbacher, 2003). Moreover, other research has shown, contrary to early Piagetian studies, that young children are inherently compassionate and that, as children age, they interpret their evolving social world more in concert with their local culture (Castelli, Massaro, Bicchieri, Chavez, & Marchetti, 2014).

From computer modeling and economic game theory to cognitive psychology and decision theory, researchers have learned much about human mental life (Weller, Levin, & Denburg, 2011). So, too, the more researchers learn the more they find themselves returning to philosophy to ask "Why?" "How do we know what we think we know about thinking?" and "What do we mean by the term *thinking*?" Improving thinking is critical to understanding thinking itself (Raeburn & Zollman, 2016). Understanding and improving thinking is key to creating and sustaining a better world for each self and each community.

Improving the self and the surrounding communities is achieved through the respect and sharing that is evident around the world through the Great Conversation of Humankind. The Conversation began in philosophy, and philosophical reflection continues to foster and prompt the sciences in their continued search for more robust truths about all that matters to humans. The Great Conversation is inherently philosophical, and that element must be preserved for STEM practices or any other educational practice to succeed in developing autonomous and competent individuals.

Philosophers as different as the pragmatist John Dewey and the idealist Matthew Lipman reminded educators that expanding the intellectual horizons of students requires apt engagement with philosophical reflection. This they rightly claim is true at every stage of development. We have created a set of scripts in the subsequent chapters of this book for professional teachers to use to help them ensure student opportunities for reflection. In the pragmatic tradition of Dewey, we have styled our approach to accommodate teachers working in restricted climates of core curricula and high-stakes standardized testing.

Dewey dreamed of a philosophically inspired curricula. Lipman was content just to gain control of a part of the curricula and dedicate it to philosophical thinking. Noble as these dreams might be, they are not realistic ambitions given the current state and national approaches to education. To develop students' thinking skills and intellectual dispositions, teachers must have tools they can insert into the curriculum at a moment's notice to take advantage of that rare "teachable moment" (Angrist & Lavy, 2009). The scripts in this book have been developed for just that purpose.

## THE NATURE OF POTENT THINKING PRACTICES

Benjamin Bloom et al., Robert Sternberg, Richard Paul, and others have produced taxonomies for identifying attributes of better thinking (Wagner, Johnson, Fair, & Fasko, 2016). These taxonomies have proven useful to researchers who want to assess and evaluate different teaching practices. This book, however, is aimed at prescribing the basis for best practices in developing student-thinking potency. We intend to be exhaustive in accounting for the range of optimal thinking practices and dispositions. This means we will address speculative wonderment, reflection, understanding, truth seeking, and finally planning and decision making. Adolescents have to do more than understand the world better; they need to plan for their role in it as well (Weller, Levin, & Denburg, 2011).

From cognitive psychology we learn that humans are born with a certain cognitive apparatus. For example, as Berwick and Chomsky (2016) note, humans seem to have a hardwired capacity for learning a native language. Of course, which native language any given person in fact learns depends on when and where they were born. Developmental psychology alerts educators to the fact that there are developmental stages that must be accommodated if thinking excellence is to proceed in each student (Gopnik, 2010). And evolutionary psychology teaches that students' motivations to learn and cooperate are part of the species' repertoire for survival (House et al., 2013; Olson & Spelke, 2008).

While children may be truth seekers by nature (Mlodinow, 2016), their development depends on curricula and teaching strategies that avoid muting that instinct (Worley, 2015). In short, potency in thinking depends in large part on refining and then sustaining student skills and dispositions by preserving the centrality of "How do you know?" and "What do you mean by the term ___?" questions in their daily lives. These skills and disposition are systemic keys to participation in the Great Conversation.

As noted above, potent thinking depends on more than understanding, truth seeking, and reflection. Potent thinking must also direct student attention to decision making, planning, and strategic negotiation practices (Mischel, Ebbesen, & Zeiss, 1972). So in preparing the scripts we had to review the burgeoning new literature in decision theory and behavioral economics as well.

Economists, social psychologists, and decision theorists joined together with philosophers to identify problem-framing practices of thinkers and their commitment to inherent goals of: competition versus cooperation, altruism versus self-interest, and satisficing versus optimizing (Bowles, 2016). The student trying to figure out how to get what he values in a social relationship at school must consider all these things (Wagner, 2011). And so it is with figuring out the uncertainties in life generally.

In any program that intends to optimize critical-thinking skills and dispositions in students, each of the above instinctual tensions must be thought through. So taking each dichotomy in order, you will discover the rudimentary rationale driving various scripts. Once you begin employing scripts in your own classroom practice you may discover you too are thinking about your thinking in ways you never previously imagined. The Great Conversation is for teachers as much as it is for students. It is intellectual egalitarianism at its best.

Framing a problem influences the decisions people ultimately settle upon. Consider the following example. Railroads were financially struggling in the 1950s. With the opening of the Saint Lawrence Seaway and a massively expanding airplane industry there was less need for railroads. The CEO of the Southern Pacific asked his management team for ideas. "Think outside the box," he demanded. Think transportation, not railroad. They did, and soon they exploited an underused idea of shipping containers that could go from ship to railroad to eighteen-wheeler. Profits went up and costs went down. Thinkers simply reframed the problem: think transportation.

Competition was once seen as endemic to the human condition. Much research was accumulated that confirmed the suspicion that people naturally want to succeed better than those around them. But once the problem was reframed in evolutionary terms it became evident that all herd animals depend on social norms for specieswide survival (Nowak & Highfield, 2012).

Game theorist Cristina Bicchierri and her team demonstrated that norms of cooperation are evident among young children and become conspicuous in adolescent societies (Castelli et al., 2014). It is important to teens to figure out what social norms govern their social world (Weller et al., 2011).

Just as cooperation is natural to humans, so too is competition. Just as altruism is common to human beings, so too is self-interest (Taylor, 2010). Both dichotomies prove to be inherent tendencies in humans all through life (Bicchieri, 2006). Learning to think better about when to let Adam Smith's "invisible hand" drive our social and economic engagements and when to absorb costs to self to benefit others is essential to personal and community betterment. Thinking these matters through inevitably brings people into the Great Conversation. Economists use games with catchy names like the Dictator Game and the Ultimatum Game to figure out how this thinking takes place.

Each of these games has been used to show human willingness to suffer costs to improve the plight of others and to punish the greedy and other communal defectors. Anthropologist Bailey House and his team, for example, showed that children from three to fourteen years old across six cultures and three continents are prosocial early on but less so when approaching adolescence if early prosocial behavior would conflict with norms of the person's local age group. Altruism then accelerated within group and lessened in response to outsiders. Students have to figure out how to continue being with others (House et al., 2013).

In a child's earliest years he or she wants it all, but evidently not to the severe detriment of another (Gopnik, 2010). Moving on through adolescence, students encounter dating, team sports, elections, and other competitive circumstances that challenge their decision-making skills. Gambling on optimizing value for each deliberate act is likely to be too costly. Economists use the word *satisficing* to designate when value likely to be secured by an act is worth the cost (Raeburn & Zollman, 2016). In social engagements this means figuring out what competitors want and what they will settle for. Potent thinkers seek equilibrium in value distribution between themselves and other competitors. Living well is always a gamble. The script on "betting" and some of the others are intended to draw attention to this sort of decision making.

The common denominator in learning to frame a problem space aptly, to balance self-interest and altruistic interests, to balance competitive interests and cooperative interests, and to balance optimizing interests and satisficing interests is always a matter of figuring out what is going on and what to do about it (Moore, 2004). This figuring out is nurtured in the Great Conversation of Humankind, but there is more to bringing students into the Great Conversation than just building upon their intellectual resources. The Great Conversation is a special social environment. It is paradigmatic of education at its best and a beacon of hope upon which to model any community.

## THE GREAT CONVERSATION AS SOCIAL PARADIGM

The Great Conversation is where people of all ages develop intellectual potency. But how the Great Conversation happens makes it dispositionally a paradigm of social interaction. The Great Conversation is certainly a community of inquiry, a place where people try to figure out things together and to share what they have learned. More than that, the Great Conversation is a paradigm of social potency.

### Community of Inquirers

Everyone is familiar with the experience of quietly sitting alone and trying to figure out a problem. Perhaps the most famous example of this is when Princeton mathematician Andrew Wiles nearly isolated himself to figure out a solution to a problem that Pierre Fermat posed 358 years before (Wiles, 1995). Other mathematicians made advances over the years, but no one could pull it all together until Wiles in 1995. This intellectual achievement was heralded worldwide and continues to be celebrated twenty years later.

Wiles did some amazing thinking. But his thinking depended in the end on several social events. First, as R. Wiley points out (2015), learning languages and even scientific protocols amounts to no more than ritualized signaling. From the alphabet song to learning to solve quadratic equations, it is all a matter at first of "See this? Do it like this." Signaling is inherently social. It is all about bringing people together in the sharing of a language and its applications.

Second, while Wiles had to be taught to share in the language of mathematics, he also read the previous work others had done to advance understanding of Fermat's theorem. Reading and thinking about what one reads is as central to participation in a community of inquirers as is talking and listening to one another. Finding answers is rarely good enough. Sharing answers for review and confirmation is critical to sound inquiry. Wiles did all of that. You too have probably done the same from time to time.

The purpose of sharing answers for critical review is to ensure that the independent thinker has gotten things right. A person can be quite convinced she has matters right, but as pop singer Amy Grant shared with one of us in an address at the 2014 Star of Hope Mission Gala in Houston, "I can be quite stubborn about those matters of which I know the least!" There is probably a bit of that Amy Grant inclination in every person. Consequently, access to a community of inquiry where others will seek flaws in the lining of one's argument as well as those of others is essential to certifying the community as an instance of the Great Conversation.

In such cooperative arrangements truth is the shared ideal, but it is exceptional plausibility experienced participants seek to grasp. Just how to secure such a sound epistemic community remains as challenging to adults as in the case of the Weighing Reasons Conference at Princeton last year (Lord & Maguire 2016) as it is to teachers trying to bring students into open and critical dialogue (Lacewing, 2015).

Again, that sharing can take place as readily in written form as in spoken discourse. The critical element is that each person offering an answer or hypothesis has prepared an argument to demonstrate coherent plausibility. The critical element in each person reviewing an argument is a laserlike focus on clarity and structure of the author's intended inference. When this process becomes symbiotic in a community an epistemic engine generates novel insights and critical caveats.

Juan may wonder if he should ask Henrietta out. She was prom queen a month ago, and three weeks ago she broke up with Juan's best friend who also happens to be the toughest kid in school. After pondering his situation for a while Juan may share his dilemma and tentative solution with a few trusted friends. Juan's safety may be involved. He could get beat up. His ego is similarly at risk if she says "no." She may not be ready to date. So many things to consider. Review of his thinking by friends could be critical.

In short, whether it is a great mathematical problem addressed by Wiles or a pragmatic social problem addressed by Juan, active participation in a community of inquirers is likely to up the odds that a plausible solution can be formulated. In the Great Conversation the resources of the community of inquiry are called upon to address big problems and not ones of local and individual preference. Wiles's challenge was certainly of that nature. Juan's had elements of big problems such as the morality of considering a friend's feelings, the value of self-interest in general, and so on.

While Juan's need for participation in a community of inquiry was essential to his life, his localized framing of the problem did not bring it into range of the Great Conversation. On the other hand, the subsidiary considerations did reach to the heights of a big problem, and perhaps most importantly the epistemic strategies of the Great Conversation were likely to serve Juan and Wiles equally well.

Certainly, idiosyncratic worries can evolve into material for the Conversation. Danny Hillis was bothered by the unsystematic way his college roommate tried to find mates for his socks. His roommate would pull a sock out of the clean laundry and then another until they matched. He threw each sock after the first back into the laundry bag! Danny figured out that with just ten pairs of socks his roommate would have to pull on average nineteen socks before he had a pair that matched! Danny figured there must be a better way.

Danny generalized the problem. He began trying to figure out an algorithm that would solve all such problems! Ah, here the problem frame became part of the Great Conversation! Here speculation about algorithms generally and critical review of previous proposals all became essential. Danny imagined an algorithm that would apply to that and many similar problems. He kept learning and pressing on in the Conversation, and he expanded on what was known about algorithms. Danny invented the famous Connection Machine and founded the Thinking Machines Corporation (Christian & Griffiths, 2016).

To sum up the characteristics of a community of inquirers, the following points seem essential. First, there must be an unrelenting demand on the part of all participants for semantic clarity. The question, "What do you mean by the term $X$?" can never be ignored. Agreeing on the meanings of terms and their use is foundational for comprehensive framing of problem spaces and evaluation of shared solutions. The scripts that follow make semantic clarity a priority.

Second, no one ever thought about anything without first making assumptions. Euclid's plane geometry was an attempt to enumerate the most necessary assumptions so rigorous proof could follow. Unfortunately, in addition to Euclid's five axioms there were many assumptions about logic that he failed to identify. In any case, the point here is that assumptions underlie all thinking. Responsible thinkers are clear about their assumptions. In a community of inquirers, fellow inquirers help identify hidden assumptions and evaluate their merit.

The scripts in this book are especially exacting, helping inquirers identify assumptions that otherwise often go unnoticed in more ordinary street dialogue. (By street dialogue we mean the flippant sort of speech one hears often in bars, sports events, parties, and so on.) While assumptions are unavoidable when thinking, responsible thinkers take care to identify critical assumptions and share their identity with other participants.

Third, call this inferential mechanics. The term *inferential mechanics* covers a lot of ground that would require a whole course in logic and one in statistics to explain. We cannot do that here. Suffice to say we mean by this term attention to avoiding common fallacies, knowing the difference between deductive certainty and all other risky arguments (Hacking, 2001), the importance of statistical caveats, judgment making under conditions of uncertainty, difference between cause and reason, truth and plausibility, and so on.

The scripts provide students opportunities to learn the application of many of these considerations without going through the exercise of learning how various formalizations created by scholars from philosophy and mathematics to computer science, psychology, and economics have attempted to lay bare the symbolic fundamentals of these inferential processes. Through their engagement with others in a community of inquirers, common inferential practices that lead to coherence and evidence-based conclusions emerge through practice (Koertge, 1998; Wainer, 2016).

## Paradigm of Social Organization

As with any community, the Great Conversation requires a specific moral architecture to ensure its success (Wagner & Lopez, 2010). The social world is populated with a variety of moral architectures in business, government, the military, religions, school systems, and so on. But the moral architecture required for robust operation of the Great Conversation is singularly unique.

First and foremost, the shared vision of those who earnestly participate in the Great Conversation is the search for truth. The notion of truth is not as straightforward as once believed, and some today even believe it to be a suspect concept reflecting authoritarian dictates of one sort or another. Neither of these commitments captures the notion of truth that unites and animates participants in the Great Conversation.

The truth sought for in the Great Conversation is an ideal. It is what participants reach for at least to the extent that they work to avoid error in their collective thinking. As a logician long ago proposed, truth is a representation that maps onto the world as it is (Horsten, 2011). This definition leaves much unsaid, such as whether there can be truth in artistic expression, music, and so on as well as whether or not there can be representations of things yet to happen or rules and actions that should happen.

For now we will just settle for the idea that truth is the ideal we hold dear when we try to get our thinking right rather than wrong about all that we undertake to think about. We accurately try to describe the laws of the universe and the laws that prescribe how we should treat one another. Participants in the Great Conversation want to get these matters right. They may disagree on what is right, but not on the importance of getting it right.

Second, the Great Conversation is the most inclusive of all human enterprises. Gender, race, religion, fat, thin, tall, short, personable, or introverted—nothing matters to the advance of the Conversation other than it leads participants away from further error in their thinking. Since each and every participant is a potential source of insightful comment or question, each participant's role in the conversation must be protected.

Protecting the participant's role in the Conversation is best ensured by focusing attention on the value of mutual respect. Note that mutual respect is not a matter of "you scratch my back and I will scratch yours." Indeed, material incentives may even frustrate the development of mutual respect and instead do no more than ensure some modest reciprocal tolerance for others and for the ideas of others. Mutual respect requires a sustained sense of sustained altruism among all participants.

Is such altruistic respect possible? In a famous study in Israel, parents were told if they continued to be late in picking their children up from day care they would be assessed a penalty since teachers had to stay behind and care for the children. After the imposition of penalties, parents routinely picked children up even later. They presumably saw themselves as simply paying for a benefit. This was contrary to the goal of getting parents to respect the teachers' time (Gneezy & Rustichini, 2000)!

Since the Israeli experiment, many researchers have shown that ill-advised incentives often create unintended consequences (Grant, 2012). Certainly in the case of introducing students to the Great Conversation the goal is to create an ambience of mutual respect and not simply a set of guarded practices based on self-interest. Mutual respect implies mutual commitment to protection of the well-being of other participants. This is one reason why the Great Conversation is paradigmatic of successful human organization.

The goal of the Great Conversation is to bring people together and not to force them together. Indeed, the history of human altruism makes it appear that in the earliest days human organization in stable communities was accompanied by the sort of altruism prescriptive of the Great Conversation even then and was essential for the successful survival of early villages in general (Nowak & Highfield, 2012). Remember, the Great Conversation is a community, a paradigmatic community of shared purpose and mutual protection (Wagner & Simpson, 2009).

Students should not be encouraged to think of this ambience as a mere commitment to free speech. It is far greater than that and more limited. Interrupting others in the cafeteria to announce your desire for a milkshake may be rude but is protected by the shared commitment to free speech. In contrast, yelling fire to create panic is not protected by free speech. The protective contours of freedom and prohibitions in the Great Conversation are a bit different.

Commitment to the shared vision of the Great Conversation is accompanied by a prohibition against rudeness or other techniques to silence or distract others. The Great Conversation invites all earnest speculations into any large-scale topic. The Great Conversation is generally not about a self-privileged person's preferences for gratification of any kind. In short, free speech, a good thing in itself, is nevertheless about me. The Great Conversation is about us and our shared world. The Conversation's prohibition against rudeness means too that students must learn virtues such as patience, intellectual tolerance, and courage to explain further their position when others confess to not understanding.

It is not material incentives that bring students into the Conversation. Presumably science has already shown that nearly every student is born with a desire to know more. When students encounter an experience of the Great Conversation they learn to embrace a community where we/they distinctions are recognized as real but of little more than inconsequential distraction. Science has shown that humans are born with an inclination toward altruism. This tendency is especially evident in their early childhood development (Bowles, 2016; Warneken & Tomasello, 2008).

In the Great Conversation, when its social commitments are fully realized, each student recognizes that every step away from error is invaluable. This means that students must find the Conversation liberating from the enslavement of ego. In other words, students learn that in the Conversation the idea is to separate oneself from error and not to enshrine one's own opinions in the minds of others. To have the fault of one's own belief revealed by another is as valuable as being able to show the weakness in another's position. This is another instance of altruistic and mutual respect.

When introducing scripts to your students, you are an ambassador welcoming them into the Great Conversation. You are the host. The party is for them. Stick to the script and never freelance your own opinion. You may always say one of three things.

1. What did you mean by the term ___?
2. How do you know?
3. Could you tell us that again in other words?

Wherever there is a question mark, stop and solicit an answer—even if the question mark appears in the middle of a paragraph. Never ask two questions in a row without getting an answer to the first question. This is all about finding flaws in early thinking, so subsequent thinking is evidently more plausible.

Never tell students that there are no right or wrong answers, because if that were the case then you are wasting their time. There are seldom right answers, but the purpose of the Conversation is to help us find and, for good reason, dispose of wrong answers—collectively. Be sure to protect quiet respondents from being overlooked by more excited participants. Remember we care about all—altruistically. Remember this is a process whose moral architecture depends systemically on mutual respect.

Never decide or let the students decide "Oh, we already addressed that." Both you and they may be mistaken about just how exhaustively you did discuss a specific matter, and that is why it shows up again (Worley, 2015). Good discussions never end. The script may be over and it is time to move on to other things, but students later discuss the ideas aroused in a good script at home with friends and family. When you are having good discussions you will hear about it days later.

Watch for how scripted discussions punctuate your classroom ambience. Do students bravely ask "How do you know?" and "What do you mean by the term___?" more often? Are parents and other teachers mentioning to you how your students raise the most insightful questions? Do students seem more courteous to one another? Do students seem more protective of the least as well as the most popular members of class?

Through the process of scripting you as the teacher should also experience the thrill of being a student once again. You should find yourself eagerly waiting for the next comment and biting your lip so as not to join in and take over with your two cents' worth. All too often we forget that the best teachers are always those who forever remain students at heart in the subjects they teach (Wagner, 1990).

Remember always that this is your opportunity to bring students into a paradigm of human community. Celebrate what you can accomplish.

*Chapter Two*

# Middle School Scripts

The scripts in this section are specifically designed to encourage experience and practice with abstract thinking and Piaget's Formal Operations. Students must be allowed to practice abstract thinking to improve and actually reach the Formal Operations stage. Having the ability to think critically and abstractly is imperative for participation in the Great Conversation.

### TIPS FOR USING THE SCRIPTS SUCCESSFULLY

- *Read the entire script before reading it to your students.* This will help you know when you need a dramatic pause or a quick follow up.
- *Be patient with your students!* Give them time to think. Many may have never had the opportunity before to think critically. These opportunities will help move them forward.
- *Never give your opinion!* Once you jump into the discussion with what you think, the "right" answer has been given, and student thinking and conversation will shut down.
- *Wait time!* Read the script/question and wait . . . quietly!
- *Use the scripts as often as possible.* Although there does not have to be a set curriculum or timeline, the more opportunities the students have to stop and think critically, the more improvements and risks you will see.
- *Make this time special.* Before beginning the scripts, have the students close their eyes and relax. This lets them know that something different is about to happen. It will seem silly at first, but students quickly begin to enjoy this break.
- *Think, pair, share.* Sometimes students are more comfortable having time to write their ideas and sharing them with a partner or small group before

sharing with the large group. This is true with difficult topics or when students are just beginning the process.
- *Fit the scripts in as an introduction to a lesson or when waiting in line.* There is no set time for critical thinking. You will find that some scripts will require a longer instructional time. Others are fun and can encourage your students to think critically while waiting for their turn in the restroom.
- *Reuse some of the scripts at the end of the school year.* This way you can really see the development of your students' thinking.

## ART

Do you know what the word *art* means? Good. So tell me what is art? What is the difference between an art and say, a craft? What is the difference between an artist and a craftsperson?

*Art* is one of those words people take for granted. Everyone from five-year-olds on up seem to think they know what the word *art* means. But when they start talking about it in a group, some surprising things happen.

Sometimes people say silly things about art. For example, someone might say art is in the eye of the beholder. Now people sometimes say that about beauty too, and there is good reason to be suspicious even about whether or not beauty is in the eye of the beholder. Whatever might be said about beauty, clearly it is not the case that art is in the eye of the beholder. Art and beauty are clearly not the same thing.

A thing may be beautiful or ugly, important or trivial, balanced or imbalanced, in harmony or not, distressing or comforting, and still be art. So, even if it were true that beauty is in the eye of the beholder, that may not tell us anything at all about what art is or where it might be found.

If you walked through a forest or a junkyard, could you spot a work of art if you came across it? Could an expert do any better walking across the same paths as you in spotting a work of art? How so?

What makes someone an expert in art? Is it possible there are no experts in art? If there really are no experts in art, does that mean there is no subject matter properly called art?

At one time works of art tried to capture the essence of something by representing a scene, a person, an act, or a thing accurately. That was true for the longest time in history.

In the last hundred years, a variety of different ways for thinking about art have emerged. Some of these ways of thinking may be right, some may be wrong, or it might just be possible that no one can tell the difference between right and wrong ways of thinking about art.

At the end of the nineteenth century and into the twentieth, artists called *impressionists* were saying that the artist ought not try to represent a thing but rather portray the impression the thing makes on the senses of the artist. Subsequent artists who called themselves *expressionists* said that artists should express the unmitigated and simple essence of a thing.

During the mid-twentieth century, there were artists called *surrealists* who thought art should reveal something about the human soul. Finally, artists called *pontillists* believed art should be done with pointlike, scientific precision capturing the light effects of nature, and others called *primitivists* said art should portray human instincts.

Most recently of all there are those who claim art doesn't have to do anything but "talk to us." No one seems to know what it means to say simply "art should talk to us," but this ambiguity does illustrate something of the mounting confusion surrounding this simple word *art*.

Should art be distinguished from accidental paint spills or bloodied operating gowns recently used? Why? Not all events are art, are they? If everything that happens is art, then the word *art* is in danger of losing all meaning. Isn't that right? Why should we distinguish art from other events? How can we distinguish art from other events?

Surrealist painter Salvador Dali once signed his name to a $1, and then was able to auction it off for $1,000. Ah, if only you and I could do that! In any case, after Dali's auction a reporter asked him if he was just putting on a great joke with his auction or did he consider the signed dollar real art. Dali said simply, "What Dali signs as art *thereafter* is art." What do you think he meant by that?

For something to count as art, does there have to be some sort of human intention involved? Just what sort of intention would be necessary for a thing or performance to count as art?

People debate over whether something is good art or poor art. How is that debate different from a debate between people about whether or not a certain object should count as art at all? Does the word *art* have any meaning to it? How do you know what someone is talking about when they use the word *art* in their sentences?

Does it make any sense to have an art museum? How do we know that what we have in an art museum from ages past is art at all? How do we know an art museum has any art inside at all? How do we know the museum has good art or bad art? Is there any way of telling one art museum is better than another?

If there is no way to tell the difference between good art and bad art, then why go to art museums? Why do we take children to art museums or major performing arts productions?

Apparently, at least in the eyes of some, there is art everywhere. If that is so, then is there any purpose in having an art museum or an expensive performance hall? If no one can know what counts as good art or bad or, if art names anything special at all, why talk about the idea of art at all?

What could you tell a visiting Martian about what the word *art* means? Is there anything more than human intention involved for something to count as art? Is human intention even necessary for something to count as art? What does the word *art* mean? Should art ever be valued? Why should anyone ever value art over anything else that seems to be lying around? Does the word *art* have any purpose in our conversations? Explain what the purpose is for our word *art*.

## AWESOME!

Have you ever heard someone say something is "awesome"? What exactly was the person saying? Is saying that something is awesome different from a sentence like, "I think I have a fever." How is it different to say something like "I think I have a fever" on the one hand and on the other hand to say that something is awesome?

To say that you have a fever is like giving a report. You are saying that in reality things are a certain way. It's like reporting that most rocks are hard, that rain can make you wet, and that people should eat nutritious food to stay healthy. To give a report is a very different sort of act from declaring your feelings about something, right?

When we talk, sometimes we report things, but other times there are other acts we perform when we talk. For example, when someone passes you in the hall and says "Hi," is that person reporting anything? Sometimes we talk to perform an act, in this case the act of greeting another. A person might just smile or wave at you and those acts would have the same meaning as saying "Hi" to you. Is that right?

So when we use the word *awesome*, do you think we are reporting something or performing some other kind of act? If the air conditioning is turned up to the highest setting, we might complain that it is too cool in here. In that case our talk would be the act of giving a report.

Sometimes, however, people used to get excited and exclaim that a new car is really cool. When people claim a new car is "really cool," do you think they are giving a report about its temperature, or do you think they are doing something different? When people exclaim that a new car is really cool, is that like saying it is awesome? How are the two acts similar?

In saying a new car is cool or awesome people are not reporting anything at all. Instead, like in the act of waving or saying "Hi," they are expressing themselves. In saying "Hi" they are expressing a greeting to another, and when exclaiming that something is "cool" or "awesome" they are expressing their satisfaction, happiness, and delight with something.

So, talking allows us to perform a variety of acts. We can report, greet, and express ourselves in many different ways through talking. Because there are so many different uses for talking, sometimes people get confused about just what they doing from one moment to the next when they are talking. For example, some people may think that they are reporting something when they are only exclaiming that something is "cool" or "awesome." What are some of the other acts people can perform through talking?

Is questioning a unique act different from any of those we have mentioned so far? Are there other examples of acts we can perform with talking that we haven't mentioned yet? Do you understand what we have been talking about? Awesome! I said awesome just now. What kind of act did I just perform? Explain your answer.

## BEAUTY

There was once a song in your grandparents' or great-grandparents' day titled, "You Must Have Been a Beautiful Baby." The song had a lyric that went like this: "Oh you must've been a beautiful baby 'cause, baby, look at you now." The song was meant to be whimsical. It made people feel happy, maybe even a little silly and giggly. The song is about visual appearance.

The song was not meant to be taken too seriously. However, we can read something more into the song. If beauty is a property of a person as a child, could the same person still be beautiful as an adult—still beautiful, despite all the changes that take place in a person between childhood and adulthood? What sort of beauty could a person have as a child and still have as an adult? Do the child and then later, the adult, still have the same beauty?

Michelangelo, a famous artist, claimed that he saw in stone beautiful forms that needed to be released from the stone. As a sculptor he claimed that all he did was chip away the unnecessary stone. He changed the stone but claimed the same beauty was there from beginning to end. Is this possible? Explain your thinking.

Another sculptor, named Rodin, claimed he created images of power, beauty, and so on through manipulating materials with his hands. (He was nearly blind.) He felt he could create meaning through his re-creation of form in bronze. In doing so, he said, he was able to create art, works of beauty. Beauty and meaning didn't exist in the material until Rodin changed the material. Through his hands, beauty came into being. Which of the two artists do you think is right? Explain your answer.

When a person changes over time, can he or she keep the same beauty all along? Even though a person changes in nearly every possible way, do you want to say he or she can still have the same beauty that they had as a child? If a person was a beautiful child and is now a beautiful adult, is it the same beauty or different? If you want to say it could be both, explain what you mean.

Could a person be beautiful as a child and be without beauty as an adult? How could that happen? Is being without beauty the same thing as being ugly? What is the difference? What is ugliness? Is it a property something or someone has? What is beauty? Is it a property some things and people have and others don't?

Can people go from being ugly to being beautiful if enough changes are made in them or . . . to them? Does this mean that a person could once have a property called "being ugly" (a property like having brown eyes) and could lose that property while acquiring another property, namely, the property of being beautiful?

Can a person be both beautiful and ugly? Can a work of art be both beautiful and ugly? Can a scene of nature be both beautiful and ugly? Do you believe beauty really exists? What is beauty?

## CONSCIOUSNESS

Are you conscious? What does it mean to be conscious? To be conscious, do you always have to be conscious of something? Can you be conscious and not be conscious of anything? How do you know when you are conscious?

Are there times when you are unconscious? When a person gets knocked out he or she is said to be unconscious. What does it mean to say that a person is unconscious when he or she gets knocked out? Is a person unconscious when he or she is sleeping? If you are sleeping but dreaming, are you conscious or unconscious? Can you remember things when you are dreaming? If a person is knocked out, can they remember things while being knocked out but not conscious? What is consciousness?

Is consciousness something that happens in a person's brain? Is there a difference between brain and mind? Brains are made up of the same DNA, RNA, and other chemical components as a liver or lung. And even though we cannot see what goes on in a liver or lung, no one supposes that livers or lungs are conscious. Why would anyone suppose that a brain is conscious? Why would some flesh be conscious and other flesh not be conscious?

When you eat sausage, you are probably eating some cow or pig brain. When you do eat sausage, why do you not experience some of the cow or pig's consciousness? If consciousness is a property of flesh, shouldn't you be able to track it just like you track the other physical properties of flesh? But if consciousness is not a property of flesh, why say it is a property of anything?

One problem with saying consciousness is not a property of any *thing* is that then we are not able to localize it. For example, if my consciousness is not hooked up to me, or if my dog's consciousness is not hooked up to him, how can we identify one consciousness with one person or one dog? How does consciousness become a part of a body of flesh? When a person dies, the flesh is still there, but the consciousness is gone. Where did the consciousness go? When the person was alive, how did we know there was consciousness in the flesh?

Our world, like all worlds, is made up of atoms and molecules, laws of motion, and so on. In such a world, how do you suppose something like consciousness emerged? Maybe consciousness doesn't really exist. Maybe we only think it exists. Is that possible? But what about thinking itself . . . doesn't thinking require a person to be conscious? Can you think of some things "sub" consciously and other things consciously?

Let's say that a person tries not to think of an old boyfriend (girlfriend), but when they go out to eat, they go to a place the two of them used to go to together. Some would say they do this because they are still subconsciously thinking about the other person. Is this possible? What does it mean to be thinking about something subconsciously? Do we have a subconscious? Does each person have a consciousness and subconsciousness? Why do we have all this stuff? Do you *know* where we keep this stuff in our flesh?

Does a person ever think "unconsciously"? Your brain tells your lungs to breathe, your heart to pump, your immune system to replicate, and you are rarely thinking about this at any time when it is happening. Yet if your brain didn't keep working on all these matters, you would die. Is the brain thinking? Is this thinking unconscious? So, what is consciousness? What is subconsciousness?

Are you conscious when thinking about these questions? What does it mean to be conscious? What do you lose when you lose consciousness? What good is consciousness to people? Consciousness seems to account for very little of what the brain spends most of its time doing, so what value is there to animals to have consciousness?

Is the consciousness of a pig or a dog the same as the consciousness of a person? Could you or I ever be conscious *as a dog*? Could a dog be conscious *as a person*? How many different types of consciousness are there? What good do the different types of consciousness do for the animals that possess them? Do you suppose all animals are conscious? Explain why you think what you do.

What is consciousness?

## DIFFERENT

The man known as the father of American psychology and the father of experimental psychology was a doctor and a philosopher by the name of William James. When he was a student, William James lived in the basement of the house of the president of Harvard University. He annoyed the house owners because he kept chickens down there for his experiments on animal behavior. You can imagine how annoyed a university president and his wife could get at someone keeping chickens in their basement, can't you?

Anyway, William James tried to figure out what it is like for a baby when the baby is first born. James said that for babies the world must be nothing more than "a booming, buzzing confusion" full of a myriad of sights, sounds, tastes, and touches. James wondered how it is that babies first come to realize that one sound is different from another, one touch different from another, one sight different from another, and so on.

Also, somehow people learn to put together a collection of sights, sounds, and touches into what they learn to call a single object. So, for example, babies learn to tie together a collection of sights, smells, and touches and say this is Mom, and another collection of sights, sounds, and touches they say is Dad. How do you suppose this happens?

We tend to take for granted the ideas of *same* and *different*. But these two ideas, "sameness" and "difference," are basic to how we make sense of the world. For example, our parents are the *same* in that they are each our parents. Being our parents makes them *different from* being our grandparents, aunts, uncles, or neighbors. Snakes and puppies are different from one another in many ways, and identical twins tend to look alike though each may have a very different personality. We just couldn't get by in this world if we didn't know the difference between "same" and "different."

Burglars are different from people who are generous with what they have. Does that mean the word *different* might mean something bad? Two pounds of sugar weighs the *same* as two pounds of salt. Is the sameness of their weight a good thing or a bad thing? In most contexts, sameness of weight isn't good or bad. It is just a report that two things have the same characteristic. There is no good or bad about it. Sugar isn't the same type of seasoning as salt. The two seasonings are different. Is that a good thing or a bad thing?

Again, in most cases being different is neither good nor bad, it is just . . . well, it is just *different*! A five-year-old boy is the same age as a five-year-old girl. That's neither good nor bad, it is just a fact about something they have that is the same. A boy is different from a girl. That, too, is neither good nor bad, it is just a difference.

Sometimes, when two things are the same it can be a bad thing, but only when other things are known to be true. For example, giving someone with diabetes the same large slice of cherry pie you give to someone without diabetes could be a bad thing. Cherry pie could make the person with diabetes very sick.

In this case it isn't the "sameness" that is bad, it is what we know about the people, qualities, and consequences that lead us to say something is bad. Sameness is never bad just in itself. Sameness is just . . . well, it too is just sameness, nothing more, and nothing good or bad. Is that the way it is with the word *difference*? Explain.

An older child gets to stay up later than a younger child. The two are different, and the two are treated differently. If you are the older child, you may think this is a good thing. If you are the younger child, you may think this a bad thing. But whether or not the differences matter or should matter is not a question about the idea of difference, it is a question about differences between people and what consequences such differences should have. The idea of difference does nothing more than point out that two things are not the same. Is it good to be different?

If you have understood what we have been saying all along you would recognize that this question doesn't make sense. It is neither good nor bad to be different. It is the things that are different, and the consequences that may follow, that lead us to judge whether or not something is good or bad.

This leads us to a very odd observation about some people. Have you ever heard someone say it is good to be different? Just being good can't be different all by itself. It can just be different. Now the consequences that result from the difference may deserve to be described as good or bad, but that means a whole lot of other things must be discussed in the process.

Have you ever heard someone say or try to act the same as others? Again, this is neither good nor bad. Saying or acting the same as others can only be judged as good or bad if we also talk about lots of other things besides the idea of sameness. Is that right?

Generous people give their property away, and burglars take property away from other people. These two types of people act very differently. Can we judge whether or not the two types of action are good or bad by focusing on the words *sameness* or *difference*? If we are to judge whether it is better to be generous or to be a burglar, we will have to do it by doing something more than just concentrating on the meaning of the words *sameness* and *difference*. What do you suppose the purpose of the words *sameness* and *difference* might be?

Do you remember how we started off talking about William James? Do you think the purpose of the ideas of "sameness" and "difference" is to help us break free of the booming, buzzing confusion that surrounded us as babies? If these two ideas help us break free from that booming, buzzing confusion, and nothing more, that would still make them two of the most important ideas we ever learn, would it not?

Can you think of any other concepts that you think are as important to our thinking as the concepts of sameness and difference? (Remember to explain why you think the concepts that you name are as important as sameness and difference.)

# EVOLUTION

Do you know what the word *evolution* means? Somebody tell me what it means. Have you ever heard a person speak of the Theory of Evolution? What is such a person talking about?

What does the word *theory* mean? What is a *fact*? What is the difference between a theory and a fact? Imagine a thing such as a stone. Are the words *rock* or *stone* about something that exists? How do you know? So, rocks and stones are *things* right? What about gravity, is gravity a thing?

Isaac Newton had a theory of gravity, and just over two hundred years later, Albert Einstein revised Newton's theory of gravity. Were they both talking about the same thing?

Are there facts about gravity? Is a theory of gravity a set of facts? Do you think a theory of gravity could be an idea about a set of facts? Do you think scientists can tell which theory is right, or at least, in some sense better than the other? Are Newton and Einstein talking about the same thing or different things?

Most scientists I talk to are happy to say that gravity exists, and that gravity is a force. There doesn't seem to be much reason to argue about that much. So, while there are details that still bother physicists about gravity, most seem content to say that it exists, it is a force, and that the force of gravity is a real thing.

Is evolution, as in Darwin's Theory of Evolution, a real thing? Is evolution a force of some kind? Is the force of evolution a real thing?

Biological scientists, as different in thought as Richard Dawkins and Stephen Jay Gould, agree that *natural selection* is the key to Darwin's theory of evolution. Did you know that?

Species survive *not* because they are the strongest but because generation after generation they leave offspring behind to carry the species into the future. *Natural selection* is the process whereby *species* die out if they possess a trait that compromises their ability to leave behind future generations. Is natural selection a force like gravity? Or, is it a description of a set of facts?

What is the purpose of a theory? Can a theory be a good theory even if it is not completely accurate? Can a theory be a good theory—for now—even if one day we discover it is profoundly wrong?

# I DUNNO

Anyone ever ask you a question to which you didn't know the answer? What did you say in response? How does it make you feel not to know something? Why does "not knowing something" make you feel that way?

Have you ever asked someone a question, and she said she didn't know the answer but then went on to say she would look it up and get back to you with an answer? *Sometimes* it's really dumb to tell someone you don't know the answer to the question but that you will look up the answer and get back to them.

Can you think of a time when it is really dumb to tell a person that you will look up the answer and get back to them? Explain why sometimes it might be dumb to tell another person you will get back to them after you have looked up *the* answer.

Where would you go to find out the answer to difficult—very, very difficult—questions? How do you *know* you can find good or truthful answers by going to that source?

Here is a set of questions that many people may have thoughts about, *but* nobody *knows* the answer to these questions. You don't need to try to answer these questions, just listen to them and think to yourself how difficult it would be to *know* the answer to each.

1. What is the best form of government?
2. What is the best economic system?
3. Is there an ideal standard for identifying true beauty?
4. Is a virus alive or dead?
5. Is there anything smaller than a quark?
6. Did the universe happen by design or by random chance?
7. What happened before the Big Bang of the universe?
8. Where do the truths of mathematics exist?
9. Is the universe made up of particles, or is it made up of little tangles of energy?
10. Which theory of evolution is the right one?
11. What is consciousness?

Did you notice that even as we went through these questions some of you wanted to talk *as if* you knew the right answer to a specific question? Since no one knows *the* answers to these questions, you were about to push off your opinion *as if* you knew what you were talking about. You wouldn't be the first person to do such a thing.

People often shoot off their mouth and talk *as if* they knew something when *in fact* they don't at all know what they are talking about. Now, there is certainly nothing wrong with expressing an opinion *as an opinion*. Intellectually *responsible* people do that all the time. Do you know what an irresponsible person is?

Intellectually *irresponsible* people talk as if they know what they are talking about when in fact they don't. There are intellectually *irresponsible* people in all walks of life. That is one reason why we all have to be careful when we listen to another person; unless we are sure the person is intellectually responsible, we need to be careful about what we accept as true.

This irresponsible behavior is especially difficult to detect when the person talking has impressive credentials in another unrelated field of study, is attractive, personable, or seemingly smart. If the person *knows* what he or she *claims to know* the person *ought* to be able to explain to us *how* he or she *knows*. Have you encountered such people? Do such people sometimes have important jobs? Are such people sometimes very influential in society? When such people are influential, is that a danger to an organization or society? Explain.

Some people get irritated when you ask them how do they know something. That is usually a sign that they haven't been responsible and really don't know if what they are saying *is* true. Respectfully asking another person how he or she knows something is a way we show that *we* are intellectually responsible people. Another way we show that we are intellectually responsible people is by always asking ourselves how we know something.

Consider the questions we mentioned before and notice how different they are from the following set of questions:

1. How many people are in this room?
2. How much is two plus two?
3. Are some people in this room taller than others?
4. Is there anyone in this room wearing glasses?
5. What is the primary function of the human nose?
6. Are there any antelope in this room?
7. Is the bare floor in this room hard?
8. Is murder (taking another person's life just to be mean) wrong?

In each and every one of these questions, we have a reasonably good procedure for determining whether or not an answer is likely to be right or wrong. But in the first series of questions there is no such procedure, at present. In the first series of questions, we might be able to figure out that some answers are wrong, but we can't identify any answers as clearly right.

For example, in contrast to the first set of questions, consider the question in the second set about the human nose. If a person did not know the primary function of the human nose, there is probably a pretty good explanation of its function in an encyclopedia or in a book of human physiology. If a fuller explanation is required, it is often possible to find further references cited in such sources, and one can always compare various sources to see if they agree on an answer.

But unlike a question regarding a function of the human nose, no scientist or philosopher can as yet give an explanation of what consciousness is, or even, why it exists. How important is it to you to have right answers to questions you ask? Explain your thinking.

When you take a standardized test you try to get as many right answers as possible . . . correct? Is the chief reason for going to school to learn lots of right answers? Explain your thinking about the chief reason for going to school. Think about this. No one ever got a Nobel Prize in the sciences, the Templeton prize in science and religion, or the Fields medal in mathematics because he or she did well on a test. Never! Doing well on a test is not what makes people smart, nor does it motivate smart people to do the things for which we award them prizes.

Every intellectual award winner is motivated by a question. They are motivated by questions that cannot be easily answered. They are motivated by questions to which no one can simply look up an answer. They are motivated by questions that are presently unanswered. There are no major prizes for "looking up answers." Since our intellectual heroes are motivated by questions, do you think it is important for schools to teach students answers to easy questions for which we have uncontroversial answers as well as teach them when and how to doubt—that is to say, teach them when and how to ask a series of sustained and relevant questions?

People in the habit of memorizing might be easy to manipulate and trick into believing false things. They might be easy to trick because they are so quick to try to memorize things that are presented to them. On the other hand, people who never study seriously and memorize very little are unlikely to have good reasons *to ask* questions when it is appropriate or to know when an appropriate answer has in fact been given.

The world's most famous scientists are usually quick to say, "I don't know" when they are asked questions for which they have no *justifiable* answer. Moreover, if the question is a really good one it may intrigue them so much they begin a study into the unknown world relevant to answering just that question. They see in such a question an opportunity to learn something new by asking further questions. They think, study, run experiments, and, when all is done, they hope they have found *truth*, or, at the very least, a better answer than anyone before had ever *fully* considered.

How do you know when to doubt something you read in a book, see on the Internet, or hear on television or in a classroom? Has anyone ever taught you effective strategies for doubting? How often do you ask yourself or others "How do you know?"

## DOUBTING AND THE QUESTION "WHY?"

The question "Why?" is not very powerful as a strategy for effective doubting since almost anything can be said as an adequate answer to that question.

Think about this for a moment. Imagine someone asks you the question, "Why did you do that?" You may answer such a question in a variety of ways.

For example, you might say: "Because I was conditioned to do that under these circumstances" or, "Because my genetic predisposition made me do it," or, "Because I felt like it," and others. But in contrast to the question "Why?" the question "How do you know?" forces the *intellectually responsible* person to think through what makes sense in the given situation before answering with just any flip response.

Another important strategy before effective doubting can even begin is to ask, "What do you mean by the term $X$?" If a person doesn't know precisely what he or she means by the term the person is using, he or she can't be sure what makes sense. Moreover, in a general discussion or shared search for answers, if people don't agree on the meaning of important terms, there is no way to guarantee shared understanding. Without shared understanding there is no way that people can knowingly come to agreement on either a question or subsequently, an answer.

What is the difference between being good at doubting and just being stubborn? What is the difference between being good at doubting and being rude during conversation with others? If you spend all your time studying for a test of so-called right answers, how will you ever learn to doubt when it's important to doubt? Can a person learn to be intellectually responsible if he or she never learns to doubt? Explain.

Why is it intellectually responsible to sometimes say simply, "I don't know"? No one knows how the Big Bang of the universe happened, so is there anything wrong with saying "I don't know how it happened" (as Nobel Laureate and astrophysicist Steven Weinberg often says) or maybe, "I don't know but I suspect that . . ." (as mathematical physicist Stephen Hawking might say) or, "I don't know but I believe that . . . " (as physicists John Polkinghorne, Gerald Schroeder, Frank Tipler, and John Barrows) might say?

In each of those cases the intellectually responsible person just fesses up to his ignorance or *acknowledges his uncertainty*, but then may share a solution he knows is only a hunch of some kind—something not yet knowledge. What makes a person an intellectually responsible person?

To be intellectually responsible, do people have to be honest with themselves and with others? To be intellectually responsible, do people have to be committed to finding truth as much as possible? To be intellectually responsible, do people have to know how and when to doubt? If you are going to become more intellectually responsible, what should you start doing?

## LAW

What is the law? Give an example of a law of nature. Why is the example you have given of a law of nature count as a law of nature? What makes something a "law of nature"? Can laws of nature be wrong? Explain. Can laws of nature change? Explain.

What makes something a "law"? In our country we have a number of "laws of the land"; for example, traffic laws. Give an example of a traffic law. What does it mean to say someone violates a traffic law? Explain how it is that traffic laws and laws of nature both count as laws.

How is a criminal law different from a traffic law? We speak of the laws that govern our nations, our states, and our local communities. These laws deal with contracts, criminal matters, the Constitution, and so on. Some law is created in our legislatures.

Some law is administrative law that is created by a duly authorized administrative agency. Much of law that governs our civic lives is common law. Common law is comprised of court decisions that the appellate level courts render and that attempt to ensure that each decision reflects the courts' decisions in previous cases; that is, the precedents. Together, all this makes up what people mean by the law of the land. In what sense are these "laws" and nature's "laws" both laws?

What is different about being wrong about a law of nature and being wrong about a law of the land? What reasons are there for following the "laws of the land"? What would happen if people decided not to follow the laws of the land?

In the Judaic/Christian tradition the Ten Commandments are said to be God's law. To violate a commandment is supposed to be to do something profoundly and controversially wrong. Are the Ten Commandments like other laws? Could there ever be anything as profoundly wrong about violating a law of the land? Explain.

Why do laws exist? What do laws do for us? Why do we sometimes find a need to change the law of the land? Presumably, most laws are changed because the sovereign authority concludes there is something morally misguided about the law as it stands. Does that mean that the law of the land is meant to serve our sense (or the sovereign's sense) of moral rightness? What is it that the law is supposed to serve?

The law of the land is a human artifact. We make it to serve our purposes. But what are our purposes in creating laws? What if we disagree on our purposes, how then should the law be constructed? And keep in mind the many different kind of laws you deal with every day.

What does the word *civilized* mean? We sometimes speak of being more or less civil with one another. We may criticize someone for being uncivil with another person. We speak of civil community. And relatedly, we may speak of doing our civic duty. What does it mean to be "civil" toward others? Lawyers tell us that the law developed as we left our primitive states of association and affiliation and became more civilized. How does the law help us to become more civilized?

## MAKING A PAINTING

Can a person make a mud pie? Can a person make a painting? Can a person make a promise? What is a mud pie? What is a painting? Does a painting have to represent something to be a painting? If you paint a picture of me and everyone says it looks nothing at all like me, have you failed to make a painting? Can a person make a painting that doesn't look like anything else and still count it as a painting? What makes something count as a painting?

A famous American painter, by the name of Jackson Pollock, started making paintings that he thought showed interesting designs, unpredictability, unexpected combinations of paint distribution, texture, and so on. Pollock's paintings don't look like anything we see in the natural world, but many people value his paintings very highly. Pollock worked very hard to get his paintings just right.

Some people said Pollock's paintings look like a rag someone used to clean paintbrushes. If someone did use one of Pollock's completed paintings to clean a paintbrush, Pollock would be very upset and probably accuse the person of ruining his painting. How could it ruin Pollock's painting if it was never intended to look like something else in the first place? Explain.

If someone knocks over several cans of paint by accident and the paints spill, running together and so on, would it make sense to look at the accidental spill and call it a painting? Does the artist have to *intend* something in order to make a painting? Explain. Now, tell me again, what does it mean to say a person *makes* a painting?

## MAKING PROMISES

We say that people make mud pies and they make promises. What does it mean to *make* a promise? People can point to the mud pies they make, and they can point to the paintings they make. Can people point to the promises they make? What does a promise look like?

Is a promise something you can smell, taste, touch, hear, or see? There is a *big* difference between talking about *what* might be promised on a given occasion and what a promise *is*. So again, I ask you: Is a promise something that can be touched, tasted, smelled, heard, or seen? Do promises even exist? How do you *know* promises exist?

Long ago there was a cartoon character named Popeye. One of his friends was a guy called Wimpy. Wimpy was always hungry and never had much money. Wimpy would go to someone working at a restaurant and say, "I will gladly pay you on Tuesday for a hamburger today." When Wimpy says something like that, is he making a promise? Explain.

If no one gives Wimpy a hamburger, then does a promise exist? Lawyers say that what Wimpy did was make an offer. There is no promise until someone accepts the offer. If someone gives Wimpy a hamburger today, then Wimpy is obligated to pay the person on Tuesday for the hamburger he eats today. Lawyers say that promises are about creating *obligations*. What is an obligation? Are obligations like mud pies or paintings? Can you touch, taste, smell, see, or hear an obligation? Do obligations exist? Do obligations exist in the same way that promises exist? Which is more real, obligations or promises? Explain your thinking.

Obligations identify the distribution of duties and the manner in which duties can be paid off. For example, anyone who makes an offer, such as Wimpy's, to pay you on Tuesday for a hamburger today is obligated to pay you on the following Tuesday for the hamburger you give him today. There is no way out of it. Wimpy and all like him are obligated to pay their debts when they make such offers and the offers are accepted. Do you understand how making promises can create obligations?

There's still a problem. We now understand that obligations are a *consequence of* promise making but, we still don't know what a promise *is*. A promise must be a very real thing because once a promise is made, obligations are created. Once obligations are created, people are blamed for not living up to their obligations. Sometimes people are even taken to court because they fail to live up to the obligations they create as a result of making a promise. But even after saying all this we still don't know what a promise is. Do you know how to make a promise? Explain how you make a promise.

As noted above, lawyers say you can tell that a promise has been made when you can identify an offer and its acceptance. This is how you can tell a promise was made but, in the present tense, how do you *make* a promise?

Linguists and philosophers study language very deeply. A famous British philosopher and linguist is a fellow by the name of J. L. Austin. Austin explained that people make promises by engaging in a ceremony. For example, Wimpy is creating a promise when he makes his offer *and* has his offer accepted by another.

It is *the ceremony itself* that makes the promise. *Saying the words*, "I promise . . ." to the evident accepting gesture of another person is all there is to making promises. (There are less direct ceremonies for creating promises and the courts call those implicit promises, but we don't need to go there today.) Promises are made but they can't be touched, tasted, felt, smelled, or heard, and yet they are every bit as real as those things that can be experienced by our senses.

How do you learn to make mud pies and paintings? How do you learn to make promises? Why do people make mud pies? Why do people make paintings? Why do people make promises?

Why do you think people first made mud pies? Why do you think people first made paintings? Why do you think people first made promises? No other animals make paintings. Humans do. Does that tell you anything special about human beings? No other animal makes promises. Does that tell you anything special about human beings? Explain.

What makes you so special that you alone among all animal life can make promises with one another? Do you think you could teach monkeys how to make promises? Even if monkeys engaged in the proper ceremony, do you think they would know they were engaging in a ceremony? Do you think they would *know* they were "making promises"? Explain.

Have you made promises to others before today? Did you know what you were doing when you made those promises? Were those "real" promises you made? Do you understand more about making promises now than you did before? Do you think you can do a better job of making promises than you did before? What does it mean to say you can do a better job of making promises now? If you can do a better job of making promises now, what does that mean about the type of promises you were making before? Were you making real promises before now?

You know you are obligated by any promises you make now. Are you obligated by the promises you made before today? Explain. Is it fair to get someone to make a promise if the person doesn't know what it means to make a promise? You can make a three-year-old promise to go to college and become a philosopher when they grow up.

Are three-year-olds then obligated to become philosophers when they grow up? Have you now learned something more about what it takes to make a genuine promise? What does it take to make a genuine promise?

## MERMAID WISHES

Imagine a famous movie star or singer who is running for political office. In a public speech she says, "Studies show 80 percent of all junior high school girls wish that they were mermaids." It doesn't matter why she said that. The point is it sounds a bit odd, doesn't it? If it sounds odd, should we think about its truthworthiness a bit before we accept it as true? How might we start thinking about whether or not it is true?

We might ask some junior high school girls we know if they wish they were mermaids, but their answers wouldn't prove anything about the truth or falseness of the mermaid statement. After all, we might find ourselves talking to a bunch of girls who just came from a movie about mermaids, or we may be in Wyoming far from the ocean and no one there thinks about mermaids. The sample of girls we may ask may just happen to be an especially unique group.

Still, asking junior high school girls we know if they often wish they were mermaids can give us a clue as to whether or not we should investigate further. The number 80 percent means that four out of five junior high school girls wish they were mermaids. If most of the girls we talk to do not wish to be mermaids, then how likely is it that we stumbled upon a whole bunch of girls who are among the one-fifth who don't want to be mermaids? Is this relevant to making a decision about the truth of the mermaid statement?

Assuming most of the girls we talk to say, "No, I don't wish I was a mermaid," we might ask ourselves some further questions. What sort of questions might we ask ourselves? Should we ask ourselves how trustworthy is this particular movie star? How is the movie star's reputation for trustworthiness relevant to figuring out whether or not the mermaid statement is true?

Should we ask ourselves why it might be true that most junior high school girls might want to be mermaids? Should we ask ourselves why it might be false that most junior high school girls want to be mermaids? How do these questions help us get at the truth of the mermaid statement?

Should we try to find out where the movie star got the information for the mermaid statement? What if someone asks her where she got her information and she refuses to answer, what might you think? What if she says she got it from the *Journal of Impossible Results*? Should we check out the journal to see if it is well respected by experts in the field? If it is well respected, where should this lead our thinking? If it is not respected, where should that information lead our thinking?

Think of the hundreds of thousands—maybe millions—of junior high school girls out there. How likely is it that a perfect 80 percent want to be mermaids? After all, in real studies by scientists, the bigger the number of things studied, the more likely it is that the percentages discovered will not be multiples of ten. Instead, they may be 82.456 percent or some such number. Should that perfect 80 percent add to your suspiciousness about the truth of the mermaid statement? Why? What other things might we do to check out the truthfulness of the mermaid story?

## RISK

What does the word *risk* mean? What does it mean to "take a risk"? What does it mean to "impose a risk on others"?

In a democracy, voters often distribute risk among the population they represent (and sometimes other external populations as well). In a family or other authoritarian structure, risk is distributed according to the direction of those in authority. Are there moral issues involved when imposing risk on others?

What sort of moral considerations are involved when distributing risks among others? Should risks always be distributed equally among all potentially affected by a particular risk?

Fairness and equality are clearly not the same sorts of things. John Rawls defines *fairness* as assigning to no one an *injurious effect* (note distinction between difference and injurious) *prior to the commencement* of an activity.

By contrast, equality just means treating everyone the same. Aristotle opined that you should treat equals equally and unequals unequally in order to be fair. What do you suppose he meant by that?

When it comes to assigning either risks or rewards, Rawls believes those in authority should think with a veil of ignorance cast over their likely role in any decided outcome. What do you suppose he means?

We seem to spend much more time worrying about the distribution of wealth and opportunity than we do about the distribution of risk. Does this practice, if it indeed exists, seem reasonable? How might one go about distributing risk fairly?

Are there moral considerations other than fairness involved in distributing risk? Are their moral considerations involved when one freely chooses to undertake a risk? What might those be? Give examples, and then explain your reasoning. Does anyone have a right to live a "risk-free" life? What is a risk-free life?

The creation of rights simultaneously creates duties in others. If Jane has a right to be free of pollutants in the air she breathes then presumably someone has a duty to maintain a pollutant-free environment for Jane. How are the rights and attendant duties of risk management to be assigned? On what moral grounds can such determinations be made reasonably?

In what sense is one person duty bound, obligated, to limit the risk environment of others? In what sense is a person duty bound, under moral obligation, to protect another person from risk?

How is it a moral question when it comes to determining how much risk is acceptable under a specific situation? Who should decide such matters? How should one go about an appropriate decision-making process for rendering such moral considerations sensible? Why should one's decisions be driven by such moral considerations and empirical assessments of risk?

Is it reasonable to define "risk" as any decision event in which there exists a *possibility* that the costs, to those affected by the decision, may be exceeded by the benefits? We can modify this further by stipulating that the costs to any one person or to all taken as a group are indexical when identifying a decision as a problem of risk (or from the standpoint of practical reason, one might say "risk management").

Costs come in many forms, as do benefits. Besides things of monetary value there are nonmonetary values that might matter as well, things such as commitment to one's sense of personal integrity, social sympathy for the plight of others, ego, personal reputation, and so on, to name but a few.

## SOCIAL SCIENCE

What is a science? Do things have to be measurable, observable, and countable to be included in the subject matter of a science? Does a science entail the use of logic and crystal-clear terminology to relate observations and ideas together in an attempt to arrive at scientifically justified conclusions?

What are social *studies*? Probably everyone thinks about the groups they are a part of and other groups they interact with, but does that make such thinking a serious *study*? Explain.

At one time or another, probably everyone thinks about rocks, water, stars, and mountains. But such thinking does not make one a geologist, a physicist, or an astronomer. It is not so much the subject matter one thinks about but how one goes about thinking that makes one a scientist.

Similarly, nearly everyone has thought about social matters before, but that doesn't mean they have been engaged in the serious study of such things. For example, Socrates, Plato, Confucius, and Aristotle thought about social matters quite deeply. Indeed, scholars learn from them even today. But no one would call these thinkers scientists in the modern sense (with the possible exception of Aristotle).

Lawyers, judges, medical doctors, philosophers, and all sorts of other scholars do social studies. What is it they all share in common, and what are they trying to understand? Does the idea of a social scientist make sense?

What is a social *science*? Economists, anthropologists, some geographers, some linguists, many political scientists, psychologists, and sociologists, some historians, neurologists, neurophysiologists, and epidemiologists are social scientists. What do they all share in common that makes them legitimate scientists?

Imagine all social scientists had true answers to every scientific question that could be asked about human social experience. Would we then know all there is to be known about human nature and human experience? Explain your thinking. If there is more to be known, what more is there? The Scottish philosopher David Hume referred to this issue as the "Is-Ought" Gap. Why should the gap between how the world *is* and how it *ought* to be concern us?

## THE PROFOUND, THE IMPORTANT, AND THE POWERFUL

Can an idea be profound? Give me an example of a profound idea. Here is an example of a profound idea. Our time is limited. No one ever won a lottery to give him or her more time. Everyone is born and everyone dies. Once lost, time is gone forever. So, is it important not to waste time, since once you lose it, you can never get it back? What makes an idea profound?

If an idea is about how we ought to live our lives or what if any meaning life might have, we say the idea might be profound. I say "might" because if we thought the idea was just plain silly we still wouldn't say it was profound regardless of what else it might be about. Can an idea be important? Give an example of an idea that is important but *not* profound.

Here is an example of an important idea that is not profound. It is important to return to the school bully the dollar you borrowed and promised to pay back last week. What makes an idea important?

An idea is often said to be important if it demands our attention. In other words, an idea is important if we are placing ourselves at risk by not paying attention to it. Can an idea be important and profound? Give me an example of an idea that is both important and profound.

Can an idea be powerful? Give an example of a powerful idea. An idea is often said to be powerful if it is very difficult to comprehend. For example, consider the following. If there is one more tree in my backyard than the total number of leaves on any one tree, then there must be at least two trees with the same number of leaves. Can you explain to me why that is true or false (assuming all my trees have leaves)?

It is difficult to figure this out, isn't it? The answer is true. It is a simple word problem, but it expresses a powerful, relational concept in algebra. The thought about "one more than the total number of" is neither important nor profound. It is, however, powerful. You have to do some serious thinking to capture the idea in your mind.

Give me an example of an idea that is profound and powerful. Give me an example of an idea that is important and powerful. Can you think of any examples of an idea that is all three? Which kind of ideas do you usually learn in school? Which kind of ideas do you like to think about the most? Why?

## TRUTHING

People never talk about truthing. People do talk about knowing. People also talk about believing, doubting, fearing, speculating, hypothesizing, reflecting, deliberating, suspecting, and so on. Each of the words in the list refers to an action that takes place inside the human mind. Each of these words also has a noun form. A person can have a bit of knowledge, a belief, a doubt, a fear, a speculation, a hypothesis, a reflection, a deliberation, a suspicion, and so on.

Truth is a noun. It names something. There is no verb form. There is no truthing. Truthing is not something that happens . . . ever!

What is it that truth names? If we can figure out what truth names, maybe we can figure out why it doesn't have a verb form. Let's start with the question, "Where do beliefs happen?" People may record beliefs and put them on CDs, in a computer, collect them in a book or article, and/or store them in a library. Where beliefs are collected doesn't tell us where they happen. Where do you think beliefs happen?

Presumably beliefs happen in minds. Any animal with a network of neurons may have a mind. So, too, some computers have minds. And even if computers do not yet have networks that you would call minds, cognition scientists assure us that one day computers will become mindful much like animals. In any case, it seems clear enough where beliefs "happen"; that is, beliefs originate in minds.

In the midst of all the minds' turbulence, beliefs of all kinds are generated. Beliefs range from mere opinions to highly prized elements of knowledge. Knowledge constitutes a special class of belief. What do you think makes knowledge a special class of belief?

At the very least, it seems that knowledge ties together evidence and various degrees of direct observation along with the testimony of others in a systematic way to generate some conclusion. Animals are said to know how to do something when their behavior leads to the satisfaction of some want or desire. Surgeons, athletes, and musicians are said to know how to execute some special skills exhibiting great expertise.

Gilbert Ryle, a noted twentieth-century philosopher, noted that humans seem to *know that* something is true in addition to *know how* to do certain things. For example, Gilbert Ryle *knew how* to think better than most other people. We can *know that* he was a good thinker. *Knowing that* aims at constructing a representation of how the world is. When a person says that "Gilbert Ryle was a better thinker than most," their sentence is a representation of somebody named Gilbert Ryle being compared to other people.

If someone says things like this about Gilbert Ryle just because they like him, their belief might be accurately described as mere opinion. When they make reference to Ryle's many books and articles, all of which illustrate the rigorous way he argues to make clear a point, their belief is elevated to something special, something we call knowledge. What makes a belief a special type of belief that deserves to be called knowledge?

Does knowledge aim at truth? What is the relationship between truth and knowledge? Does knowledge need truth? Does truth need knowledge?

If knowledge aims at truth, then *truth* is the target. If truth is the *target* then truth must exist outside the process of coming to know. Truth must sit beyond the process of selecting right-minded beliefs that we can call knowledge. If truth sits outside knowledge, then truth must be different from knowing and knowledge both, right?

How is truth different from knowing and knowledge? Is truth a special type of representation? What makes truth a special type of representation?

A famous logician, Alfred Tarski, once said truth is a representation that maps onto the world without evident error. What do you think, is truth a representation of facts? (The word *facts* here is referring to how the world actually exists.) If an intended representation fails to show the facts of the world as they exist, we say the representation does not count as truth. So what does count as truth? How are knowledge and truth different? Can there be a truth that no one believes? Explain.

## WHAT IS MORALITY ALL ABOUT?

Is morality about performing the right behavior? Is morality all about having the right beliefs? Is morality all about thinking in a certain way? Is morality all about how you are genetically coded or culturally determined? Is morality about conventions of social etiquette? Does morality matter to human social engagements? How so? What do you think morality is about?

In Japan, at the close of a successful business deal, people may stand and bow toward one another in a show of respect toward the other businessperson's honorable dealing. In the United States, people may stand and shake hands with one another to show respect for the other's work in completing a deal. Is this the sort of thing, bowing and shaking hands, that morality is about? Explain your thinking.

In some cultures, it is acceptable to chew with your mouth open; in other cultures it is not. Are these rules of etiquette, or are these moral principles? Have you ever heard the expression "When in Rome do as the Romans do"? What do you suppose that means? Do you think it means that if you want to fit in, if you want to get along, you should go along? Are there sometimes reasons for following the social conventions of another culture other than a desire to blend in to get along? What might be some of those reasons?

When Japanese bow or Americans shake hands to complete a business deal, could there be a deep, symbolic meaning to such behaviors other than just bowing or hand shaking? Could the deeper meaning of hand shaking and bowing be to show respect for others and the honest transactions that they completed with one another?

Many historians speculate that hand shaking began in Western Europe as a way of showing that approaching warriors meant no harm toward an approaching stranger. Isn't signaling to another person that you mean him no harm a demonstration of some moral commitment?

In some cultures, bowing is standard social convention. In other cultures, hand shaking is a standard social convention. Could it be that these two very different social conventions are meant to make public each person's commitment to show respect toward the other?

Respect, by its very nature, is a foundational moral commitment. Respect is something inside a person directed outward to others or to institutions or policies and laws. Respect is not a behavior. Do social conventions of etiquette sometimes make it possible to show one person's moral commitment to another person? Explain your thinking.

Social conventions of etiquette are local. In contrast, foundational moral considerations such as respecting others seem often to cross geographic and even historical borders. What makes moral considerations special? Explain your thinking.

*Chapter Three*

# Secondary School Scripts

The scripts in this section are specifically designed to allow the high school student the opportunity to practice thinking critically and abstractly. The more opportunities students have to practice this type of thinking, the more they will improve. The more students improve, the more they are able to contribute to the Great Conversation.

### A WOMAN'S WAY OF KNOWING

Have you ever felt really bad about something and none of your friends seemed to know why? People may have noticed you were behaving a little differently but thought nothing of it. Sometimes when that happens does it seem that your mother catches on and she asks what's wrong, or maybe just helps you in some special way that mothers understand? Some people think that when things like this happen it is because women have a special way of knowing. What do you think?

Imagine a boy named Jed who might have lied "once or twice" when he was a kid. He knows it wasn't the right thing to do. He knows it now, and he knew it then, but the darnedest thing used to happen. Sometimes he could get away with a lie to his mother, but it was much harder to get away with a lie to his father. Do you think that is unusual?

Since his father was better at knowing when Jed was lying than his mother, do you think that means men have a special way of knowing?

Do you think whether you are male or female makes any difference at all when it comes to knowing something? I am not asking you to consider whether boys or girls know *more* than the other. All that I am asking you to think about is whether or not you think *knowing* is a different sort of thing for women than it is for men. Is it different for a woman to know $2 + 2 = 4$ than it is for a man to know that $2 + 2 = 4$?

Do women do a better job knowing *about* some things than do men? Explain. Do men do a better job knowing *about* some things than do women? Explain. (Remember this is *not* the same question that you just answered.) Would it make any difference to the world if men were better than women in knowing about some things and women were better than men in knowing about some other things? Explain. Who knows about men better, other men, or women? Who knows about women better, other women, or men?

Marie Curie is a famous physicist. She won the Nobel Prize in physics in 1903 and the Nobel Prize in Chemistry in 1911—not even Albert Einstein did that. (Of course, Einstein's work was largely theoretical and Curie's work was experimental.) Do you think that when Marie Curie knew about facts in physics she knew about them differently than men who knew the same facts? Explain.

We can't ask Professor Curie about how she did her thinking. She died long ago from radiation poisoning. She and her husband (he shared one of the Nobel prizes with her) used to pick up pure radium in their hands. In those days, no one knew how dangerous that element could be. They both died from the effects of their scientific work. In a sense, each was a hero of science. They risked their lives to pursue truth and to gain more knowledge to share with all the world. They will forever be remembered for their genius *and* their courage.

Although we can't ask Professor Curie about her thinking, there is another woman scientist almost as famous as Professor Curie. Professor Barbara McClintock won the Noble Prize in medicine for her scientific research in genetics.

She was interviewed often, and there are several wonderful books about her life. She got annoyed when interviewers asked her if a woman's way of knowing in science is different from a man's. She says, "Of course not." Science, she said, is the most equal and democratic thing that humans ever do. It doesn't make any difference what your gender is or where you are from in the world, either you know something or you don't. Do you agree with Professor McClintock?

Professor McClintock never had children, and she never got married. She dedicated her whole life to science. She, too, was another scientific hero sacrificing everything to pursue truth. Although Professor McClintock didn't have children of her own, she certainly had parents. Do you think her father knew things about her that her mother could never fully understand? Explain. Do you think her mother knew things about her that her father could never fully understand? Explain.

Is science a special type of knowledge? Do you think Barbara McClintock is right when she says it is the most democratic knowledge of all? What is there about scientific knowledge that makes some people fall so in love with it they sacrifice everything in life just to learn more science? Do you think you understand much about what it's like to be a real scientist? Typically, doctors and engineers are not considered scientists. What do you think it means to be a "real scientist" like Albert Einstein, Marie Curie, Barbara McClintock, or Stephen Hawking?

## HILARY PUTNAM'S "BRAIN IN A VAT"

Hilary Putnam is a very famous philosopher who spent a long and very productive career doing philosophy at Harvard University. One of the most interesting questions he raised has since become the basis for several Hollywood movies. Putnam was concerned about how we know what we *think* we know. How do you think we come to know things?

Putnam asks us to remember that every bit of data we have about the world comes to us through our senses. Through touch, taste, smell, sight, and hearing we collect data. When we see a desk something happens with light on the surface of our eyeball that begins a series of electrical and chemical events that goes from the surface of the eyeball along a road called the optical nerve and into the brain. No one has a picture of a desk in his or her brains.

If a neurosurgeon opens up the brain of a person thinking of a desk, the neurosurgeon will find no movie screen or television screen inside the brain showing a picture of a desk. Once information goes from the eyeball to the brain, it gets translated into an electro/chemical language that only the brain understands.

The same is true for all our senses and all the data they send to the brain. So, Putnam wonders, how can we know we are really seeing a desk? How do you *know* you are seeing a desk? Every bit of information you have about the world gets translated electrochemically before you ever get a chance to think about what the data mean. How do you *know* you are drinking a soda or swimming in a pool?

Putnam asks us to imagine the following: a mad scientist gets your brain and puts it into a vat. The vat is full of nutrients, and so the brain is kept alive. The mad scientist has discovered the electrochemical language of the brain itself, and so he sends into your brain all the scenes, tastes, smells, sensation of touches, and sounds that fill the brain with a complete image of participating in the real world. (Putnam's ruminations here eventually became fodder for several Hollywood movies, the most famous of which was probably *The Matrix*.)

How do you know that that hasn't already happened to you? How do you *know* you are *not* a brain in a vat?

We never experience the world as it is when we are thinking. All we experience is our thought about the world and the sensations we think we are having about the world. How can we ever be sure that what we *think* about the world matches how the world in fact exists?

Do humans shape the world through their actions? How do you know? If we are brains in a vat, we could be led to think mostly anything. We could be *caused to think* we are making our own decisions and that our decisions matter to what happens next. Yet all along we could be brains in a vat living in an artificial world created by a mad scientist. Can you give me a single good reason to think that we are more than just brains in a vat? Explain.

How do you know the other people you think are in the world are not just created images by the mad scientist? Is there anything you can do with your mind that a mad scientist could not cause to happen to your brain while it is sitting in his vat of nutrients all wired up to send you electrochemical messages?

There is a difference between dreaming and experiencing the world. Does that help you think about the difference between being a brain in a vat and being a brain inside a real body that moves about? How does the difference between dreaming and having real experience help?

Can you remember the most real dream you ever had? In the middle of that dream did you know you were dreaming or did it seem like everything being dreamt was real? How do you tell the difference between vivid dreaming and reality?

What would someone have to say to you to convince you that you were a brain in a vat? Would it be difficult for someone to convince you that you are a brain in a vat? Why is that . . . is it just because you are stubborn or too ignorant to know any better? Why would it be so difficult for someone to convince you that you were nothing more than a brain in a vat?

How do you know you are not a brain in a vat?

## CHANCES ARE

What if I tell you that if you flip a perfectly balanced coin ten times, the chances are it will land on heads five times. Would the chances be any different if the coin was not perfectly balanced? Why?

Suppose your friend gives you a coin. He tells you he has measured the coin in every way possible, and that it is perfectly balanced. He tells you if you flip the coin ten times the chances are that you will get five heads. To see if he is right, you flip the coin ten times. Much to his surprise, the coin turns up heads all ten times.

Suppose your friend is so disturbed about what just happened that you have to try to calm him down by explaining how such a strange thing could happen. What might you say? For one thing you might say that the coin isn't perfectly balanced. When your friend said the coin was perfectly balanced, he was expressing a statement he strongly believed to be true.

However, one of his measuring instruments could have been broken. He could have been clumsy when performing one of the measurements. In short, lots of things by themselves, or in combination, could have caused him to draw a mistaken conclusion about the coin. But does that mean chances are the coin was, in fact, not perfectly balanced? What should you say to him?

Suppose you try the experiment again. You flip the coin ten times and this time you get ten tails! You and your friend are astonished! The coin *can't* be balanced toward heads and then get ten tails. What might you suggest to explain this situation to him?

Your friend is confused at this point, so he asks you, "What are chances *about*, anyway?" What might you say to him in return? Can chances change from one experiment to the next assuming everything else stays the same? It is important to consider the fact that in the first experiment we got ten heads and no tails, and now in the second experiment we got no heads and ten tails. Why?

Suppose now you insist on running one more experiment. This time you flip the coin one hundred times! You get ninety-nine heads and one tail. Now, with a perfectly balanced coin this result is unlikely. So does this experiment show without a doubt the coin is not perfectly balanced? Why or why not?

Could the coin be perfectly balanced but this result is just an unlikely coincidence, a chance occurrence? What *is* a "chance occurrence"? When something occurs that you don't expect, how do you know if it was just a "chance occurrence" or if your original expectation was mistaken in the first place?

Imagine a perfectly balanced coin. Since this is not a real coin but only a thought experiment, we can simply insist the coin is perfectly balanced. If we flip the coin once, it must land with either heads or with tails up. There is a 50 percent chance heads will show up and a 50 percent chance that tails will show up. What *kind* of a chance is this? Are the chances here real?

What *are* chances? Do they exist in the mind? Do they exist in nature? Do they exist in a world of reason? Is there a relationship between *causes* and *chances*? If you know all the causes, can an *unexpected* chance occurrence still happen? Are chances caused just by gaps in our knowledge?

## DESIGN

We talk about dress design, architectural design, engineering design, and organizational design. What does the word *design* mean? Properly speaking, do engineers design automobiles, ships, planes, and trains? Describe something you once designed. Be specific and detail all the events that took place in order for you to complete your design.

Is designing something the same thing as "making" something? Explain. Have you ever spilled something and made a mess? The mess you made happened by accident. What happened was just "by chance." There was no design involved. Is that right?

So, sometimes we *make* things by accident, and sometimes we *make* things by *design*. What is the difference between *making something by accident* and *making something by design*?

What does the word *intention* mean? Is intention always involved when something is made by design? Are things like purpose, plan, deliberateness, and willful desire all a part of making something through design? Explain. Are any of these things *necessary* when making something by chance? Explain.

What if you were to knock over a bucket of paint onto a framed, blank canvas by accident? You wipe off the frame, but you let the paint on the canvas itself dry. You figure you'll throw the canvas out later, since the canvas is ruined.

Later, when you return, you find an art critic admiring what he thinks is your "painting." He says sincerely he thinks that you are another Jackson Pollock. Jackson Pollock is an American painter who specializes in nonrepresentational art. What do you think about the art critic's comments? Does the painting he is looking at show that you have great promise to be an artist? Should the framed canvas be thought of as a painting at all?

To be a work of art, does a canvas with paint on it have to be *designed* or can it just be a messy accident that worked out well? Things can be made by chance, and they can also be made by design. How do you tell the difference between the two? Do you think a standard mousetrap, with spring, metal bars, a platform, a place for bait, and so on could be made by chance, or do you think at least some effort at design must be involved? Explain.

Think about the human eyeball and visual system. Do you think the eyeball could happen just by chance? Explain. Do you think some design had to be involved in the design of the eyeball?

Some evolutionists believe that the eyeball and visual system came about by natural selection operating on chance variations. Since with all the animal species that ever existed there have been only two designs for eyes and vision, some evolutionists believe there are rules and constraints built into evolution just as there are rules and constraints built into physics. Not everything happens by chance. Still others think there are other reasons for things being as they are. What do you think?

What are the sorts of things that can be made purely by chance? Explain your thinking. What are the sorts of things that can be made only by design?

Describe some things that you think are made somewhat by chance and somewhat by design. When you observe something, how do you decide if it was made by chance, designed, or made by some combination of the two?

To say that something is made by design, does that mean it is *better than* something made by chance, or does it just mean there are different ways things can be made? Is the discussion you are being led through something that was designed by an author, or has it all happened by chance? How do you know? Have you participated in some discussions that seemed to develop partially by chance and partially by design? Give an example and explain what your example illustrates.

What sorts of things must a designer have in mind to create a design? Is a designer responsible for all the consequences of his or her design once it comes into being? Explain why or why not. Why do you suppose the art critic could not tell the difference between the accidental mess and a real painting?

How do you know something has happened by *chance*? How do you know something has been *designed*?

## FRIENDSHIP AND AUTHENTIC GIFTS

When a holiday like Valentine's Day approaches, the nature of a true gift provokes more serious thought than at any other time of the year. With a twinkle in their eyes and often, promotional checks in their pockets, celebrities declare in each and every case how wonderful it is to *get* gifts. They may even recommend crass formulas for gift giving such as how much a suitor should spend of their annual income to purchase an engagement ring.

Mothers, preachers, and schoolteachers once taught that it is the thought that counts, and, moreover, that it is better to give than to receive. So, who is right? The possibility of taxonomizing gifts is a very practical exercise. Just as Aristotle showed with the concept of friends, a simple taxonomy can serve many practical purposes. For example, in the case of friends one such purpose is to identify what sort of friendship is the most worthy of pursuit, and under what circumstances. And of course, the pursuit of friendship often leads to gift giving so the two topics are related, are they not?

In the case of friends, Aristotle spoke of friends of common interest, friends of common motivation, and friends of shared well-being. *Friends of common interest* are those who are naturally attracted to the same sorts of things such as knitting, shopping, football, and ultimate fighting contests.

*Friends of common motivation* actively pursue a goal shared in common with others. Such friends may constitute a neighborhood investment club, a gang, the Enron management team, a church mission group, or any other association where the wheels of common pursuit are greased by amiable camaraderie.

Finally, *friends of shared well-being* are the rarest and most valuable of all. Such friends feel they experience the triumphs and tragedies of those they call friends as much as they do their own triumphs and tragedies.

Gifts can be taxonomized hierarchically from the lowest to the highest as well. There are gifts of common purpose, gifts that are ugly, and gifts that are beautiful. *Gifts of common purpose* are those most often seen. These include gifts of social obligation such as a wedding gift to the son of a distant relative, tips, simple thank you gifts at the close of a deal, Secretary Day gifts, the company's annual United Way Drive, or, in short, any gift made in the effort to keep things running smoothly.

*Ugly gifts* are much different. A gift is ugly not on the basis of appearance, price, custom, or substance. For example, when a friend's mother died he found in her jewelry box an acorn on which his father had scratched out his love for her. The father had given her this amazing gift at a time during the Depression when he had no money. This gift was of humble appearance and yet priceless—but only to the mother. The friend doubts his mother ever thought of any other gift as more substantive, and she certainly thought it was anything but ugly.

What makes a gift ugly is the intent of the giver. Ugly gifts are meant as a down payment on the soul of the person gifted. Ugly gifts are meant to enslave or at the very least ensnare the will of another to the purpose and intention of the giver. Oftentimes the more attractive, costly, and conventional the gift the more it rightly raises suspicion in the mind of the recipient. An ugly gift leads to the benefactor's claim that the recipient is in the benefactor's debt because of the size of the benefactor's largesse. Ugly gifts are not the sort of thing one ever receives from what Aristotle counts as a true friend.

So when Valentine's Day approaches, eyes turn away from gifts of common purpose and certainly away from gifts that are ugly and toward *gifts that are beautiful*. Just as intent makes gifts ugly, it is intent that makes gifts beautiful. The intent that makes a gift beautiful is the sole and exclusive intent to make life a bit better for another person. There is no expectation of something in return or turning the other's will to the benefactor's way of thinking.

Mother Teresa and Jimmy Carter are known for the beautiful gifts they give others through their charitable works. Neither tried to make their most beautiful gifts known for any purpose of personal gain, they just did the things they did at times to make life genuinely better for others—no strings attached.

Lovers should be friends, true friends, the truest of all friends in Aristotle's sense. True lovers, just as true friends more generally, can only give gifts that are beautiful. The intent of the gift is to make better the life of the beloved. The giver wants nothing more. The giver doesn't seek self-satisfaction; what is done is done for the good of the other.

Beautiful gifts last a lifetime. The friend's mother had her acorn for fifty-one years. As she grew very old she gave away much of her jewelry to friends and family. There was never any question that the acorn, rotted out from the inside, was far too beautiful to ever give away. The friend now has that acorn. This beautiful gift reminds him always of the love that surrounded him as a child. The acorn was an anniversary gift. One cannot imagine a more perfect Valentine's Day gift under the circumstances.

The same friend also volunteered for a year at M. D. Anderson Cancer Center in Houston, Texas, and he saw there many beautiful and romantic gifts. He saw the gift of a lover's hand holding the hand of the beloved, a beloved who feared that all was lost save for the expressed love of this truest of all friends.

Jewelry stores, fine restaurants, hotels, travel agents, and car dealerships may fear the effect on the bottom line if the above taxonomy of gifts is taken seriously. After all, such businesses make money whether the gifts purchased for Valentine's Day are of the beautiful or ugly sort. But price is no measure of beauty or ugliness.

Consider a recently married rich man. Insensitive, materialistic sorts may imagine all the stuff he may give his new bride. Yet a personally inscribed acorn may express for the rich man all the beauty that it did for the friend's father and mother. It is the intent that matters, and only the intent.

Intent isn't easy to discern. It is revealed through circumstance, integrity, sincerity, imagination, and the unmitigated desire to contribute to the well-being of another. Remember, Valentine's Day is named after a saint. Valentine's Day should be about good people giving beautiful gifts to the uniquely special people in their lives. This is not a "gifting day" like most others wherein gifts of common purpose prevail.

Valentine's Day is especially unique in that it alone is about beauty, a beauty that is singularly in the eye of the beholder. On Valentine's Day, it is the beauty of the gift that should tell the story of all that is relevant between the giver and the gifted. Too often, however, ugly gifts will tell a very different story on this day. What story will be told on your Valentine's Day?

## GENES

By now everyone has heard of genes. Genes are the instructions coded in DNA to create proteins responsive to the unfolding environment around an embryo, fetus, infant, child, and even the full adult.

A scientist has proposed that if the Shroud of Turin is authentic, we could get a snippet of Christ's blood from it, and then clone the Savior. What do you think about that? In principle, if you can get a snippet of undamaged DNA, then presumably there is no reason why one day you can't create a being that is a carbon copy read out of those genetic instructions. But would you be re-creating the original, or in this case, would man be re-creating the creator?

The short answer is "No" in both cases. There is a type of twin known as mirror-image twin. They are far rarer than identical twins. Their DNA is the purest match imaginable. But from the very beginning with cosmic radiation and other environmentally destructive forces affecting the coded DNA, even mirror-image twins are not two of the same kind of thing.

Shared DNA leads to a lot of commonality. Not just physically, but even emotionally and psychologically. This should not be a surprise since emotions and thoughts and other psychological events seem to originate in a piece of tissue we call our brain.

No Christian thinks that he or she is nothing more than a piece of animated flesh. We have souls, and no DNA can code for such a thing. Just as no DNA can code for our souls, no replication of DNA can give we creatures the power to re-create the creator. At best, we could run off a copy of a body, a body He originally made incarnate. There is no DNA for the incarnate, and all can rest assured there never will be.

Science is capable of extraordinary things, but we should have learned our lesson in the wake of *The Da Vinci Code* by Dan Brown not to be lured into every wild story someone claims to be the newest secret insight into the meaning of life, religion, or anything else of grand importance. Real scientists are used to making modest claims. When you hear people in the name of science or anything else announcing wildly improbable claims, just remember the gullibility of the unwitting sheep that fell victim to the silliness of *The Da Vinci Code* fabrications.

## GOVERNMENTAL PURPOSE

Is there a purpose to government? What is *the purpose* of government? Some people answer this question the way some people answer every question. They say simply that everything is different and everyone is different.

Then, without much thought they say again, every government has a different purpose. But when someone says something like "Every government has a different purpose," this indicates the person isn't thinking very carefully about the question asked. The question did not ask, "Do governments have purposes?" Instead, the question asked, "Does government, *as an institution*, have purpose?"

This question is like asking if the practice of medicine has a purpose. It does. It has the purpose of healing the sick. Individual doctors may have a variety of purposes for why each works in medicine, but the *practice of medicine* may only have one justificatory purpose; namely, healing the sick. So, let's try this again. Does the *institution of* government have a purpose?

Traditionally, attempts to describe the nature of government are divided into two camps. One is called the classical theory, while the other is called the liberal theory. Let's look at the liberal theory of government first. The word *liberal* does not mean what television journalists mean when they speak of liberal versus conservative. In fact, many of today's so-called conservatives are adherents of what has traditionally been called liberalism.

The liberal tradition says that government should govern as little as possible. Its primary function should be that of, say, a referee or an umpire. People gather together in a state so each can pursue his or her own happiness as long as it doesn't interfere with the happiness of anyone else. The purpose of government is to let each person *do* what he or she wants to do without colliding with the actions of another. For example, a liberal theorist might argue that people ought to be allowed to ingest any drugs they choose as long as such behavior doesn't lead to any immediate harm to someone else.

Long ago in China there were places called opium dens. People went there and behaved as they wished out of the eyesight of others, and presumably out of harm's way. Is there anything wrong with the government creating such a place for the use and protection of its citizens? Explain your thinking here and be careful to stipulate that such centers could be safely managed so the users cause no immediate harm to others. Is it okay for a government to stay out of people's personal affairs as long as those affairs don't have immediate limiting effects on the affairs of others?

What if frequent drug use makes a person dangerous to others later in life, say ten years later—Should government anticipate such long-term consequences? What responsibility does government have to potential victims ten years down the road? What if, in a seemingly random fashion, recreational drug use only makes some people dangerous ten years later; should that matter to government now? What is governmental responsibility all about with regard to its citizens when considering such matters?

How could a government ever know all the long-term consequences of each act for each individual? Should a government only worry about short-term consequences it can reliably identify? Explain your thinking.

The liberal tradition says the purpose of government is to ensure each individual optimal opportunity to *do* whatever she or he wants to do. If an individual's recreational drug use is unlikely to cause problems for others, then the government should not interfere with such individual behavior. What do you think? Is the real reason that people have government to protect their freedom to behave as they wish?

Thomas Hobbes and Jacques Rousseau, two social contract theorists and founders of the liberal tradition of government, believed government was put in place simply to protect the exercise of select freedoms. If a government cannot fulfill that purpose for its citizens, then the government ought to be abolished. What do you think?

Notice that the discussion we have been engaging in has nothing to do with what *form* of government is best. There is a reason for that omission. Before anyone can begin a discussion of what form of government is best, he or she must first figure out, generally, the purpose of government.

A contrast to the liberal theory of governmental purpose is the classical theory. The classical theory of government (also called the natural theory of government) dates back to the ancient Greeks. For example, Aristotle thought that people were destined to naturally come together in community. It is in our nature to do so, Aristotle claimed. It is not a choice.

Consequently, since people are inevitably brought together by their very nature, the purpose of government must be to help people fulfill their nature. Government, in short, must help people become all that they can be. Liberal theorists, too, think people come together for a reason; namely, that people desire security for the exercise of personal freedom and the opportunity for personal pleasure. How do you see these two ideas of governmental purpose differing from each other?

In the second and third centuries AD, some people went out to the Egyptian desert to live as hermits and pray to God. In a relatively short time, they developed networks with one another and rules for getting along. Soon thereafter, they began the first monasteries in the West.

The liberal theorist may not envisage any reason at all for people desiring to be hermits to ever come together in communities. The classical theorist by contrast would say the evolution from hermitages to monasteries was inevitable given the nature of human character. The point, say classical theorists, is that getting together is as natural for people as breathing. Like wolves, people are pack animals. So what is the job of the human pack?

Because people get together naturally, the job of the state, say classical theorists, is to help each person *flourish*. The best pack of wolves is the one wherein most wolves are well fed and leave behind ample progeny for the next generation.

In contrast to the wolf pack, the human pack seems designed to do a bit more. A good state, as the U.S. Army once advertised, helps each person become *all* that he or she can become. A good state discourages people from throwing away their lives in idleness or drug use and encourages people through state-controlled education to "exercise each of their excellences excellently" (again, as Aristotle once said). Do you think this classical (natural) theory of governmental purpose is right-minded, on target so to speak? Explain your thinking.

Should people have a right to throw away their lives if they choose? The liberal tradition says they do, while the classical or natural tradition says they do not. To help as many people as possible become fulfilled, the natural tradition acknowledges it may be necessary at times to mistreat an individual if that treatment would truly increase the likelihood that the overwhelming majority would flourish in every possible way.

If one individual has the single unique set of genes that could be developed to save all humankind from the onslaught of AIDS, then to the classical theorist it would be permissible to hold that person against his or her will to study the genetic makeup that may one day be exploited to save millions of lives. In contrast, the liberal tradition would normally not allow the exploitation of such an individual. The liberal tradition says the individual must always come first, and the state should exist only if it protects and makes people happy. What do you think?

What is the purpose of the state? Both traditions cannot be fulfilled by the same state. Explain why not. Which tradition do you think comes closest to getting right what the institution of government ought to be about?

## GOVERNMENTAL PURPOSES AND THE FOUNDING FATHERS

John Kennedy's "Ask not what your country can do for you, ask what you can do for your country" is an example of the classical tradition. Martin Luther King's "I Have a Dream" speech is similarly a classical statement. Each asserts that a good state should result in each of us living in harmony with the other without distraction and showing respect toward all. In other words, there are some goods of human relations that a good state ought to make universal.

The classical tradition places the state first. Classicists believe that good states make good people—each of whom may then flourish in respectable and respected fashion. Ultimately, the flourishing of the many benefits nearly everyone, and so the likelihood of beneficial evolution is all but guaranteed.

In contrast, the laissez-faire of so-called Reaganomics is an example of traditional liberal thinking. If Reagan was a liberal thinker, what do we call liberal thinking today?

John Adams, who preceded Jefferson into the White House, and who was part of the committee of five who were assigned the task of writing the Declaration of Independence, wrote, "A good state should seek the greatest possible happiness for the majority. To do this the state must be based on a foundation of moral virtue." Clearly, Adams sounds very much like a classical theorist—especially if we flesh out his meaning for the term *happiness* (clearly it has some connection to moral substance of some kind).

Adams's successor to the White House, Thomas Jefferson, took a different tack. When writing the Declaration of Independence, he wrote, "We hold these truths to be self-evident, that all men are created equal . . . (Abigail

Adams was astonished when Jefferson spoke these words because as she wrote to her husband, John, how can he advocate liberty for all while holding slaves? [her own father was a Massachusetts slave owner]) that they are endowed by their creator with certain inalienable rights."

Here Jefferson declares in the spirit of the liberal tradition that the state must protect the individual's "life, liberty and the pursuit of happiness" (happiness here seems to mean simply fulfillment of desires). How do the Aristotelean (classical) and Jeffersonian (liberal) notions of happiness differ here? Which is the right theory of happiness for helping us understand the nature of governmental purpose?

Aristotle says that in a good state "each is able to pursue his own excellences (Note: what is an excellence?) *excellently*." For Aristotle, such exercise is self-actualization—the foundation of happiness. By way of contrast, what do you think Jefferson meant by "the pursuit of happiness"? Did he mean that each person gets to do whatever makes him or her feel good as long as it doesn't interfere with someone else pursuing similar idiosyncratic delights?

Interesting to note here that Aristotle and Jefferson each had some notion of democracy as the best form of government, but each had very different notions of the purpose of government. The U.S. Constitution sets up a representative democracy meant, in the words of the Preamble, to "form a more perfect union, establish justice, insure domestic tranquility, provide for the common defense, promote the general welfare, and secure the blessings of liberty to ourselves and our posterity."

This seems to echo the spirit of both the liberal tradition and the classical tradition of government, and these multiple purposes may be in tension with each other. For example, providing for the common defense has on several occasions meant drafting people to serve in the armed forces—whether they were willing to or not.

But can we find any clue to what the framers of the Constitution thought in how the Constitution came to be ratified? Many of the Founding Fathers would not ratify the Constitution without including a set of ten amendments known today as the Bill of Rights. The first six amendments protect you and me from all the rest. These six amendments echo the concerns of traditional liberalism. So what do you make of this fact?

Clearly, the Founding Fathers recognized the perils of being on the horns of a dilemma. *There is no eclectic position.* Do you suppose the Founding Fathers tried to use rhetoric that simply appeased everyone and yet did nothing to settle the matter of governmental purpose? Why would they do that?

In the absence of an eclectic position, the Founding Fathers attempted to balance two traditions. On the one hand, they sometimes tried to make the well-being of the individual the priority. On the other hand, they also said the well-being of the state matters most when it is trying to maximize the good for all. Inevitably these two commitments must come into conflict with each other. When they do, they again force into the open questions about the very purpose of government.

The Founding Fathers hoped that a good government could *balance* commitment to the two purposes. But hope is unrealistic. What happens when an imbalance between the two purposes occurs? How can an imbalance be fixed? In the end, must not one commitment be realized as more important than the other? Which commitment is generally more important? Is it possible to sustain a balance regarding governmental purpose over the long run? Do we seem to be in balance now or not? If not, which commitment seems to have the edge in contemporary American political thinking?

Is one *form* of government more likely to sustain a balance between the two commitments better than other forms of government? If so, which form of government is most able to sustain such a long-sought balance? How do you know such a form of government is able to sustain such a balance? If such a balance is unattainable, then which commitment should we endorse as having highest priority? Explain why. Which form of government is likely to sustain such a commitment?

If government had no purpose, how can the state sustain itself over the long run?

If government had no purpose, then as liberal thinker, Thomas Hobbes says, every individual would be in peril. The liberal thinker, Hobbes, is willing for government to foul up from time to time as long as it usually manages to protect most of us in the enjoyment of our liberties most of the time. The classicist in contrast says a good government should do more . . . it should make us better people.

A liberal theorist, strictly speaking, would be against any and all funding for what we know as public education. Each person should be free to educate himself or his children as he feels is appropriate. In contrast, the classicist dating back to Aristotle thinks that the state should play a role in education. The classicist thinks the state has the duty to help as many citizens as possible to flourish. This, in turn, further enriches the state. Where do you think liberals and classicists would come down on matters of public health funding?

So again, should government aim at making each of us secure enough to pursue his or her own delights, or should government attempt to make each of us all that we can be? What should be the purpose of your government? What is your obligation under such a government? What is your neighbor's obligation under such a government? What are your governmental authorities' obligations under such a government?

## Chapter 3
## IDEA ENZYMES

In biology, enzymes are a type of chemical that can cut up a molecule. Let's think about an "idea enzyme." An idea enzyme cuts up complex ideas. Idea enzymes divide and separate ideas. Take a simple idea like tolerance.

The Reverend Martin Luther King Jr. drew a line in the sand. He said some things are wrong and some things are not. For example, he said all people should be *tolerant* of all adult citizens casting a vote during an election. He said that all people should respect other people's right to be a customer at a business or to sit rather than stand on public transportation.

When Reverend King said things like that he was telling the world that people should be *intolerant* of those who would deny other citizens their right to vote. He was saying people should be *intolerant* of those who would close off their business to others because of race. Are you getting the idea? *Tolerance and intolerance represents a concept that serves as an idea enzyme.* It separates human thinking about what is okay in treating others and what is not okay.

Censorship is another example of an *idea enzyme*. Censorship says you cannot censor some things but you can censor others. For example, in the United States, you cannot censor a family that is quietly bowing their heads and saying a prayer before a meal at a restaurant. On the other hand, you can censor someone from yelling "Fire" falsely in a crowded movie theater. Can you think of some other concepts that count as *idea enzymes*? Give an example of a concept you think is an idea enzyme, and explain why you think it is an example of an idea enzyme.

Is the concept of rights and duties an example of an enzyme idea? Is it *possible* to create a right for someone that does *not* create a duty for someone? If someone has a right to vote, then are there not others who have a duty to not interfere with the exercise of that person's right? Explain how you think rights and duties work. Do you think rights and duties are an example of an idea enzyme?

Idea enzymes are not merely words that contradict one another. True and false *contradict* one another. But true and false are not the same sorts of thing as rights and duties. The first represents contradiction. The second is an enzyme idea example. What do you think makes the two different from one another?

When a person contradicts themselves people around them usually recognize the contradiction and say so. For example, if a person says, "I need an hour to think about this but sixty minutes won't do," people may object saying the person is contradicting herself. In contrast, if a person says, "We should be tolerant of loud cheers in the auditorium but not whistles," people may ask, "Why do you want to draw the line there?"

How does this contrast help you understand the difference between idea enzymes and contradictions?

## INDUCTION AND BLACK SWANS

Induction is a way of figuring things out. No one quite knows how to best do induction, but statisticians, social scientists, and philosophers are all working on the challenge.

Induction starts by making observations, and then summing up the same type of observation in order to decide on something we know or at least probably know. For example, imagine you have a friend, let's call him Festus. Festus has a habit of embellishing stories, and even making things up and telling people his stories are true. Festus has done this so often that you may decide that he is dishonest, or more directly, a liar.

Now this doesn't mean you think he is always lying, but the odds are so high that you are not likely to believe him. You have made an induction. You went from many examples that you thought were of a similar kind to a decision about a whole class of events (Festus's falsehoods) to a conclusion about the source of those falsehoods (Festus).

Many things can go wrong when making an induction. It is difficult to figure out the best way to make the best inductions in each situation. We will not talk about many of those today, but you might think about it on your own. Today we want to talk about induction and black swans. Sounds funny, doesn't it? Why would we talk about black swans? I will tell you why!

A famous expert in the study of induction, Carl Hempel, used swans as a favorite example. Imagine a scientist trying to describe the nature of swans by just looking at them. They have yellow beaks, wings, long necks, webbed feet, and are white. Well, at least all the swans he has seen are white. To be sure he's right, he travels the world to see swans wherever they live. He has seen over a million swans, and they have all been white. Does that mean he can now say that he knows all swans are white? Explain your thinking.

Now, as it turns out the next day after he is through with all his swan studies, he goes for a walk in a nearby park and there with some other swans is a swan that looks like all the rest but it turns out to be black! What should the scientist think? Should he insist all swans are white, and so this bird cannot be a swan simply because its color is different? Should he just say, "Oops, I made a mistake. Not all swans are white."

What if he figures things out inductively using natural frequencies and says simply, "All but one in a million swans is white, the other is black." Will this be a more reliable decision he can reasonably share with other scientists?

How will he know that tomorrow he will not find a dozen swans and they will all be black? Can a person know anything for sure if he figured things out inductively; that is to say, can you know something for sure if you just look at an enormous collection of samples but not all the members of a population, here, now, and forever?

David Hand, a statistician, says what we can know inductively are two things. A large sample collected just right will tell you much about a population the sample is from. In Hempel's example above, Hand would say we know most swans are white, and we know that there are sure to be nonwhite swans on occasion because we already found one in our extended sampling.

Hand does not answer whether or not we can know whether or not the ratio of black swans to white will always be one in a million. So, do we know anything important or not?

Hand says we know that there will be a rare black swan. When things are uncommon, it doesn't mean they don't happen. It means they don't happen often, but they are sure to happen sometimes.

During any day lots of coincidences happen around the world. They were each bound to happen sometime. It is just that because they are so rare, we get surprised when they do happen. Hand says uncommon happenings are as natural as common happenings, they are just less frequent. What do you think? Should we expect rare things to happen? Should we stop being surprised when they do happen? What should be our attitude toward the unexpected when it happens?

An applied mathematician, Nassim Taleb, said that no matter how good we are at figuring things out inductively, things will still happen that no scientist or other expert could ever have anticipated.

In contrast to Hand, who thinks we can know that certain specific events will occur, however rarely, Taleb thinks there will be things that happen that we couldn't have imagined no matter how good our inductive thinking. He calls these wholly unpredictable events "Black Swans." Taleb thinks that we cannot know the unexpected will happen as Hand thinks. Instead, he thinks all we can do is prepare ourselves for the general idea that the unimaginable will happen and we will have to deal with it as it does. Who do you think is right?

Think of global warming. Hand seems to think that scientists can know a list of things that are likely to happen because of global warming. Taleb thinks global warming exists but some things that happen are beyond scientists' powers of inductive thinking. There will be no way to anticipate them. Instead we will just have to concentrate on becoming better thinkers so when the unimaginable happens we will do a better job of recovering from it.

Can you think of better ways to think inductively than just deciding Festus has been lying for the past two weeks, so Festus will always lie to me?

## KISSING

There is a song from long ago, sometime before World War II, that says, "A kiss is still a kiss." What do you suppose that means? What is a kiss? What does a kiss mean? People sometimes briefly kiss as a greeting or to express other emotions as well. How many different emotions can a kiss express?

When you smile, you may express to everyone around an emotion of pleasure. But kissing allows you to express an emotion only to the object kissed. So kissing limits your emotional attention to just one object or person. That makes kissing a very special act. What else makes kissing such a special act?

A Catholic may bend her knee, bow her head, and kiss the ring of the pope as a sign of respect. This is a common practice when a person meets the pope. In Blarney, Ireland, there is a castle, and high up in the tower there is a stone in the wall called the Blarney Stone. People kiss the Blarney Stone for good luck. They hope that by doing so it will give them skills that will make it possible for them to talk anyone into anything. People also kiss when greeting one another. In each of these cases, the kiss means a special one-to-one relation exists between the kisser and the kissed. Why is that so important?

You can wave a greeting to a whole crowd, but you can only kiss one person at a time. What is significant to you about that fact? Parents, aunts and uncles, and grandparents kiss their children, nephews and nieces, and grandchildren for other reasons than just to greet them. A child hurts himself falling down, and his mother kisses the hurt place. Why does she do that? Why does the child often feel a little better after the kiss? What do these kisses mean?

Sometimes people think about kissing another person because they are attracted to him or her. Such a kiss is a romantic event. What do such kisses mean? A person may kiss his or her own hand, a mirror, or even a pillow, each in an effort to learn how to kiss another person romantically. Do those kisses have any special meaning? Sometimes when one person kisses another it feels just like kissing your own hand, a mirror, and so on. There is nothing romantic about such kisses. Why is that? What makes a kiss a romantic kiss?

What makes a kiss a really special and romantic event? Why do you suppose people kiss one another romantically? What do such kisses mean? Can people lie about what such kisses mean? Is it ever wrong to kiss? Can a person be wrong in thinking a kiss means something romantic? If people misunderstand the meaning of a kiss, can that lead to people getting their feelings hurt? How so? Is it ever wrong to hurt another person's feelings? *Why* is it wrong?

When two people who know each other well and are attracted to each other finally, deliberately kiss each other hoping the person kissed will feel very good about the experience, what is happening? What do such kisses mean? These kisses feel much different than the other kisses we have talked about. What makes these kisses so different? Do these kisses *feel* so different because of what they *mean*? Or, do kisses just feel good all by themselves? Do kisses that have meaning have better feeling associated with them? Do kisses feel better the more meaning they have?

When kisses lose feeling between two people, what happens to the meaning? What happens to the feeling of a couple's kiss if the kiss is *meaningless*? Can a kiss have a wrong meaning? Give an example of a kiss with the wrong meaning. How do you make a kiss *meaningful*? How do you make a kiss *meaningless*? Do you think some people try to kiss others without even knowing the *meaning* of what they are doing? How do you know your kisses have meaning? How do you know that when another kisses you that the kiss has meaning for the other person?

Can kisses have right and wrong meanings? How do you know whether or not a kiss has the right or wrong meaning? Anyone can smush lips together. What do two people have to know to kiss meaningfully? Would you ever want someone to kiss you in a meaningless way? Why? Why not?

Is it wrong to kiss people in a meaningless way, or should kisses always have meaning? How important is it to understand the meaning of kisses? Do you think some people have difficulty understanding the meaning of kisses? Why do you suppose some people have difficulty understanding the meaning of kisses? Do you think there is a lot to learn about the meaning of kisses? Why do you suppose meaningful kisses feel good?

Poets and philosophers as well as other scholars have spent a lot of time trying to understand the meaning of kissing. Why do you suppose it is so important to scholars to understand the act and meaning of kissing? Do you think it should be important to most adults? Why?

## LOVE, ROMANCE, AND VALENTINE'S DAY

Valentine's Day prompts thoughts of love and romance. While love and romance are related, they are not the same. Mere romance is full of sizzle and spark. Love trades sparkle for depth and breadth of shared insight. Love involves deep friendship. Potent psychological elements such as mere friendship, guilt, pity, nostalgia, or the approval of friends are no substitute for loving friendship!

Romance is related to love in that it buys time for a couple. Time is necessary for love to emerge from romance. Love must be tested, tempered, and hardened for the protection of the couple. As the intensity of romance becomes intermittent in its expression, it gives each party an opportunity to collect his or her thoughts. Each must consider whether or not together they have what it takes to *be* lovers. If love is their shared destiny, the lovers create a new social and economic unit they call "we."

The transition from mere romance to love is difficult because it requires each person to look very hard into himself or herself and not just into the other.

The central element of love (as opposed to mere romance) is the capacity to give, to be altruistic to others, especially to the beloved. This is true of all loves and not just romantic love. By contrast, in mere romance what looks like giving is often a tactic for getting—that is, for securing control over another.

In a merely romantic liaison, one person may dissolve the relationship before the other senses it has run its course. Often, the jilted party desperately tries to renew the relationship. The jilted party does this not out of love but out of something that feels far more intense, the loss of face and the desperate need to recover self-esteem.

In contrast, when lovers break up, each is left with the haunting feeling that something is still amiss. While apart, each still functions as a part of the original "we." From time to time each continues looking at the world through the eyes of the other. To want to see the world through the eyes of another is an exemplar of the kind of giving love requires. Parted lovers retain this instinct for sharing insight with one another. Again, by way of contrast, in mere romance, each party settles for getting the other to see the world the way he or she does.

Why do lovers part? Why do others never find anything but mere romance in their quest for love? One guess is lovers never part—not really. Their relationships may get derailed for a variety of reasons, but a couple with the right stuff nearly always retains the capacity to function as a "we" whether or not they ever return to one another's arms.

They never leave each other wholly out of their respective hearts and minds. It is a tragedy for such couples to let divorce or some other transient social barrier keep them apart. There may be unrequited romantic interest, but there is no such thing as unrequited love. Love is nothing if not reciprocal.

Again, in contrast, for those who never get beyond romance the problem may be that they never learned to see beyond *self*. There have been many psychological studies over the past twenty-five years that show that people who focus on *self* are routinely unhappy and an obsession with *self* often leads to depression, panic attacks, and a host of other psychological problems. People who focus on others or on tasks at hand tend to be generally happier than the self-obsessed.

People who try to control and appropriate others—no matter how polite and clever their tactics—never find in themselves the true giving that is the foundation of love. The giving of love is a truly altruistic giving. It is giving without expectation of return, prior negotiation, or reminder to the other of all that has been "given" in the past.

People preoccupied with *self* will be unable to imagine even the possibility of such giving. In their world all that is given is given to secure some personal benefit for *self*. They live in a dog-eat-dog world, so it is unsurprising they never find love despite their expressed desire to do so.

Society, generally, and Madison Avenue advertisers in particular, encourage each of us to become greed machines. Madison Avenue depends on creating in people endless streams of wants and dissatisfaction with what they have. The world Madison Avenue and Hollywood create is not conducive to something as ennobling in the human soul as love.

For many of us, it takes something as dramatic as a terminal illness to remember what matters most in life. Some time ago, a friend volunteered at M. D. Anderson Cancer Center for a year. He pushed around a cart filled with books and magazines once a week for patient use.

He learned so much from cancer patients and their families about giving and love. It was there that the friend learned that cancer can bring romantic love back into the life of a couple. When a beloved gets cancer, the lover forgets all past faults, for both know they may well lose all that is really important in their lives. On occasion, the friend who volunteered walked into rooms where the healthy person had climbed into bed with the patient just to hold the other and treasure the moment.

In contrast, he saw couples, who though married, surely had nothing more than a long past romance to unite them. In those cases, the spouse without cancer bolted from the relationship declaring in oh so contemporary a fashion, "I am not a bad person. I just can't handle this. Sorry, but I have to think of myself." There is no beloved and lover in these cases: only a married couple wherein one abandons the other at a time when the other's need is greatest and the *opportunity* for true giving is endless.

Love is not easy to come by. It deserves thoughtful and considerate attention by those privileged to enjoy its graces. To experience love you must know how to give unselfishly and how to truly treasure the gifts given to you. For example, the tears of a beloved during a moment of tenderness are more beautiful and dramatic while gracing a cheek then any jewelry adorning a throat or a wrist.

If you are truly seeking love, then know that on Valentine's Day your greatest joy will be found in the face of your beloved as he or she reacts to your offering of that "perfect" gift. Keep in mind, however, what counts as a perfect gift. If you are wealthy, then giving a single rose may be a far more profound, deliberate, and hence meaningful gesture than having delivered three-dozen roses.

If you are poor, three-dozen roses will speak volumes to your beloved. In each case, if your beloved has the right stuff, your beloved will understand fully the depth of your giving. When the two of you come together in this fashion it may well signal that together, you have a future. Happy Valentine's Day!

## PROBABLY VERSUS PROBABILITY

Are the words *probably* and *probability* alike or different from one another? Explain your thinking please. Before we began this discussion I thought at least one person would probably think the two words were different. Notice the word *probably* that I used here. The word *probability* wasn't even in my thinking. Each word seems to have something to do with the likelihood that something will happen. So what is the difference between the two words?

Have you ever played the game "Rock, Paper, Scissors"? Scissors cuts paper. So the hand signal for scissors wins over the hand signal for paper; paper covers rock so the hand signal for paper wins over rock. Rock breaks scissors, so the hand signal for rock wins over scissors.

Do you think you can probably beat all your classmates in this game? What evidence is there that might lead you to think you can beat all your classmates in the game? Maybe you are pretty good at the game. Maybe you could beat everyone here. But most of us think your evidence for this claim is suspicious. We want to know how do you KNOW you can beat each of us.

There is a national competition called the Rock, Paper, Scissors USA Annual Competition. Each year one person wins the competition and all others lose. There are experts who have studied the best strategies for winning. How do you think they studied the game to come up with the best strategies? Here's how they actually studied the game.

First they asked national champions how they tried to win each game. They made lists of all the ideas the champions shared. Then, the experts watched people play thousands of games. They would ask each winner about their strategy and then match it to the list they got from the champions. Can you figure out what the experts were trying to do? Tell us what you think the experts were trying to do with this way of gathering evidence.

The experts didn't want to just get things probably right. They wanted to find out the probability that one strategy might be better than another. They added up the number of wins that matched each strategy the champions listed. These numbers told them the probability that a strategy would work when compared against others. Probability thinking is a way of assigning numbers to what is probable and even what might be merely possible. It usually takes a long time to observe and add up what is seen and figure out a mathematical probability that something will happen.

Sometimes it is easy. If we take a perfectly balanced coin and flip it high into the air, what are the chances (that is, another way of asking what is the probability) that it will end up heads? If you said 50 percent you are right. Since it is a split, 50 percent heads and 50 percent tails, anyone who said the chance was probably heads or tails would be wrong. Probability tells us each is equally likely and neither is more probable.

Experts often try to find probabilities when making decisions. Nonexperts just try to figure out which decision seems to "get it right." What is the difference between the two ways of thinking? What is a "probability"?

## RISK II

Rights and duties are intimately related. Neither can be created without simultaneously creating the other. For example, in a democracy, Smith's right to vote is accompanied by a duty on Jones (and all others) to do nothing to interfere with Smith's exercise of his vote. But there are risks. What if the candidate Smith might vote for is a bigot, a hater, a monster of some immoral sort, should the duty to allow Smith to vote be aborted in such cases? Risk involves making oneself or others vulnerable in some sense. To what extent is it morally right to undertake such risks?

When is it morally okay to step in and make a decision for another person? Making decisions for other people is called the problem of *paternalism*. We make decisions for infants and the mentally disabled all the time. In fact, we may hold people responsible for not making right-minded decisions on behalf of a child or a mentally disabled person.

Making people responsible for the care of others is a way of designating duties. If there are duties designated, then we know that there are people who have certain rights under those designations. To ignore the rights of others, that is to say, by being lax in our duties toward others, we are said to be culpable of moral wrongdoing.

So, when is it right to let others take on certain risks? What criteria should be referred to when deciding another has a right to take on certain risks? What criteria should determine if we have fulfilled our duty to protect another from undue risk? What gives one person a right to impose a risk on others? Why might those others have a duty to accept the risk?

Imagine a nuclear waste site is being sought. It probably won't be built near the rich and famous of Hollywood. Is it better to build it near the lower middle class if it creates jobs and greater economic security? When and how should this be decided? Perhaps it is important to put the waste site away from large centers of population. But why should a minority of people be placed at risk because they live in the country and are few in number? Who has a right to determine who should be subjected to various risks?

Few medicines work on everyone for the disease for which they are prescribed. All medicines carry some risk of side effects ranging from the merely annoying to crippling effects—even death. Who should decide what risks a patient should undertake? Do probabilities matter in making such decisions? There is overwhelming evidence that neither patients *nor doctors* understand statistics well enough to make reasonable decisions in most medical situations.

Doctors know about treating diseases, not about statistical likelihoods of side effects, survival versus mortality base rates, and so on. Patients know about their fears, and not much more. Reasonable decisions in such cases demand attention to the utility of undertaking some risks in order to achieve some personally valued reward.

But who should—who can—make such decisions in morally responsible ways? Wherein does the fabric, the moral fabric, of risk analysis play itself out in terms of the distribution of rights and duties and protocols for morally right decision making? Does the fact that most people are ignorant about the moral foundations of risk decisions suggest that only a select few make decisions for all? This is Plato's philosopher-king. What are the alternatives? How important is security and happiness when balanced against vulnerability to harm?

## THE GOOD LIFE

What is "the good life"? If someone has mindlessly bought into so-called postmodernism, deconstruction, critical theory, or any other "pop" version of nihilism, they probably don't even know how to begin answering such a question intelligently.

If they have been indoctrinated into postmodernism they simply learned to repeat over and over again things like, "That's all subjective," "It all depends on your family," or "It all depends on which culture you were in when you were brought up." There is no fact of the matter in response to the question, "What is the 'good life'?"

So, the question to them is "How did you get to be so smart? How do *you know* there is no fact of the matter in response to such a question?" In the days of antiquity, the Greeks defined philosophy as the search not for knowledge but rather for *wisdom*. What do you suppose they meant when they distinguished wisdom from knowledge? Can a person know more than another person? Can a person be wiser than another person? Can your answers to each of the previous questions be profoundly right or profoundly wrong? Explain your thinking.

Some people seem to mindlessly chant that "all is relative to culture or upbringing" and so on. They seem dogmatically opposed to any other consideration. Such one-line chanting misleads and misdirects people from taking up some very important issues. For example, evolutionary psychologists theorize that it is in the species' best interest to find a satisfactory niche in nature. They often add that the best life for any one individual becomes what allows the individual to replicate himself or herself.

In contrast to that conclusion, many biologists and economists argue that evolution focuses on the survival of a species and not on the survival of an individual's progeny. To these scientists, the best life is defined by nature as what will lead an individual to contribute to the evolutionary flourishing of a community. In evolutionary terms, a community flourishes when it deals with its surroundings in a sufficiently satisfactory fashion to allow its members to live long enough to ensure its progeny a place in the next historical epoch.

For the evolutionary psychologist, it just isn't true that the answer to the question, "What is the good life?" is relative. Nor do evolutionary biologists or economists working in the area of evolutionary morality believe the answer to the question of the best life is simply a culturally relative consequence. Each of these scientific communities tells us that an evolutionary understanding of the species tells an awful lot about the "good life" for all.

For the psychologist, nature is "red in tooth and claw" (in the words of Alfred, Lord Tennyson) and one is best advised to act out of self-interest. There are no "ifs, ands, or buts" about it. For the biologist and the economist there are a variety of cooperative strategies that we ought to each learn if our species is to survive. And again, there are no "ifs, ands, or buts about it." There is no reduction to "it's all relative or how you were brought up."

Do you think you have a good idea of what might be the best life for you to live, or do you think you have just mindlessly accepted what the people around you have told you? If you are just a product (it's probably best to read that as *prisoner*) of your culture, then how could you even be reflective when answering this question? So again I ask, do you have any sound basis at all for how you are choosing to live your life at the moment? Explain your thinking.

Biologists and economists aren't the only ones who think they have found clues to the best life humans should be living—that is to say, if all things go well for the person in the natural domain. Some neuroscientists have begun finding hardwiring in the brain for all sorts of human behavior ranging from language acquisition to moral sympathy. And some neuroscientists have gone even further yet. Some neuroscientists believe they have found brain centers that when acting in concert bring about a religious experience, an experience that has been written about in all cultures, across all historical epochs.

Every culture has tried means for tagging into this state of mind. Is this state of mind an element of the good life? Explain.

The Nobel Prize–winning neurophysiologist in medicine a few years back, Sir John Eccles, believed that he had found where the soul interacts with the body. (Obviously this is not what won him the Nobel Prize!) He believed the soul interacts with the body through the terminal buttons that populate the axon, extending out from a neuron toward another neuron to make a synaptic connection. *If* there is a soul, should this be a consideration in your thinking when calculating what counts as a good life? Explain.

Utilitarians like the English philosopher Jeremy Bentham believe you should maximize pleasure and minimize pain for all. And this they say is what the good life is all about. Do you think this is what the good life should be about? Explain.

Each of the three or four positions above represents a powerful and credible solution to the problem of ascertaining what is the good life. If we can't decide between them, does that mean there is no good life to seek? Or, does that mean we aren't smart enough to solve the problem?

In addition to the positions above, religious thinkers have detailed answers to the search for "the good life." Do you know so much as to declare all these people wrong? Again, how did you acquire such powerful knowledge?

Do you think some people suggest there is no such thing as a good life because *they* aren't smart enough to figure out what is the good life, and so their default position is to say it's all relative, one answer is as good as any other? Explain.

How would you justify a claim to know that there is no one good life for all but that each has his or her own good life? This is a powerful claim to make. Do you have the intellectual material to make good on such a powerful and universal claim? Do you know so much as to declare all these people right, albeit in their own idiosyncratic way? If you do, let's hear your argument now.

Plato thought the good life was doing what you were cut out to do. Artists could only be fulfilled if they became artists, warriors warriors, philosopher-kings philosopher-kings, and so on. What do you think about this idea? Do you believe each person has a personal destiny?

If each person has a personal destiny, then presumably the good life would be to fulfill that destiny. But how does one learn what that destiny is? Where does such destiny come from, that Plato thought you were made of a metaphysical-like substance that uniquely suited you for one lifestyle and no others? A choice to act out any other lifestyle could only be made out of ignorance. You are what you are, nothing more or less. Do you think Plato had a sense of the good life? Is there anything wrong with his line of thinking? Have you failed to find the good life if you don't act out your mettle?

A talented writer fails to live the good life if he or she makes millions as an actor instead of becoming a writer. Plato would say such a person has made a mistake and misspent his life. Many people fear they are making just such a mistake when they go through what is popularly called a middle-aged crisis. Is there anything in this idea of destiny that you think is revealing about the nature of the good life?

Aristotle thought there was an answer to how to live the good life. When each person learns to exercise his or her excellences, *excellently*, then each has acquired the good life. Because each person has separate capacities for theoretical and practical reason, each will wind up living a different life, but all share one goal of exercising one's excellences, *excellently*. If a person chooses not to seek such a life, the person has, according to Aristotle, missed out on the good life. What do you think?

The Epicureans thought happiness is what we all seek by our very nature. What makes one happy is what makes for a good life. First and foremost, among those things that make us happy is being in sufficient control over our lives to choose what makes us happy.

Long before Oprah, Dr. Phil, Dr. Schlesinger, or Dr. Brothers, Epicurus told the world happiness is a *choice*. If you let others tell you what makes you happy, then they have control over you. This may make them happy, but in such cases you can never be happy—not really.

Don't place your happiness in anything that can be taken from you, Epicurus warns. If a jug makes you happy, and it breaks, then your happiness has been taken from you. Don't place your happiness in such simplistic material things over which you have no ultimate control. Does this sound like a good idea? Do you think this might be part of the answer to the question "What counts as the good life?" Explain.

If I give no thing and no other person the power to make me unhappy, then I have optimized my opportunity for happiness. Now, this has become almost a mandate of contemporary "pop" psychology, but it is nothing more than a restatement of the Epicureans' position. The Epicureans had a good run. Indeed, that is why we still study them today and why some counseling psychologists sell their advice as their own (calling it "therapy"). But if the Epicureans were on to such a great way of seeing the world, why haven't we all bought into it? Is there anything wrong with the Epicurean position?

Existentialists such as Albert Camus and Jean-Paul Sartre think there is no meaning to life other than the meaning we ourselves create. They go further and insist that we are under a moral imperative to create meaning in our lives. But the existentialist insists, no one can tell us whether or not the meaning we create is right or wrong. What do you think? Is this effort to create meaning part of the secret to a good life?

What is meaning? How do we know when we have successfully "created" it? Before we "create" meaning in our lives, what do our lives consist of? Does it make sense to speak of a meaningless life? Does it make sense to speak of a meaningful life? What makes a life meaningful? How do we know a life is meaning-*full*?

At least the Epicureans and Utilitarians encouraged us to seek happiness as the best way to live. Do the existentialists have any positive advice to offer? The existentialists thought authentic life begins with existential despair. Existential despair is the realization that life has no meaning other than what we create for ourselves. What is so despairing about that? How would an existentialist describe the good life?

Epictetus was a stoic. He was also a Greek slave. He thought all that a person has of value is his exercise of free will. If a slave master begins to bend the slave's arm, Epictetus would advise the slave to say, "Master if you keep bending my arm it will break." The slave has no choice about what happens to his arm, so why should he worry? It's a decision the slave master must make; let him worry.

The slave protects himself by not trying to control things that are beyond his control. Modern-day advocates of Alcoholics Anonymous have embraced this thinking and given a religious spin to it through what they call the Serenity prayer. Moreover, commentators have long acknowledged the strong influence the Stoics had over St. Augustine and many other Christian thinkers. What makes stoicism so similar to what you know of Christianity?

The Stoic rightfully claims that a person may have no control over what happens—even to his or her own body. All that a person can control is his or her own will. If you understand that your will and decision to interpret things in positive ways is all that you can control, then you will always be free, and it is freedom that is what makes life meaning-*full*. Neither aggressor nor disease can make you miserable unless you allow it.

The secret to life is taking control over your own will and realizing the autonomy such control affords you. This too sounds like advice Dr. Phil and Dr. Laura along with a lot of pop psychologists would give today. What do you think, is this "taking control over your life" a part of the good life?

Is there one thing you each agree must be a part of the secret to life? Why can you agree on at least this one thing? Was it worth the effort to discuss what this one thing might be? Is this one thing something we each *ought* to teach our children? Should we teach this to our neighbor's children? Should we try to teach this one thing to all future generations? What have you learned about possible answers to the question, "What is the good life?"

## WHY BE MORAL?

Why be moral? Imagine you are living in a self-sufficient community of forgiving people. The community is finally well off and so no one has to work unless they want to. Everyone has just a little bit more than he or she needs to get along. Everyone leaves his or her door open, and money lying about. There is no limit to their trust.

Imagine you could steal just a bit from various people and no one would know. Even if they did know they had been stolen from this forgiving group of people would just assume the thief had a good reason to steal and they wouldn't attempt to find the culprit. Do you think you would be tempted to steal in such a situation? Do you think others would be tempted to steal in such a situation? Would you steal—at least on occasion—in such a situation? Explain your thinking.

In the situation described above, everything is quite pleasant. Even if one person is so driven by self-interest to steal from others from time to time, it has little effect on either the social or economic well-being of the community, so why should any individual be moral in such a situation?

Many economists talk about something they call *reciprocal altruism*. By this they mean that intuitively people know that if one person starts stealing or otherwise not living in a cooperative manner, sooner or later others would as well. That's just human nature. They say actually it's more than human nature. Among many pack animals, reciprocal altruism is the norm. It's what makes a pack resilient in the face of an outside threat, and the species recognizes this fact.

So, among many pack animals, self-interest is tolerated only to a point. If it gets out of hand, the forces of reciprocal altruism kick in, and the pack unites to restore order. Is this the sort of thing that answers for you the question, "Why *be* moral?" Explain.

Economists aren't the only ones who think this way. Biologists have noticed reciprocal altruism among several species as well as other forms of altruism. Biologists notice, for example, that sometimes an animal will sacrifice its life for others of its kind, thereby sacrificing as well its opportunity to leave behind children of its own.

In the evolutionary theory of Thomas Huxley, nature was assumed to be vicious, "red in tooth and claw," yet the sacrificing of one's life to save others—especially when they are not directly related to you—suggests an unselfishness in nature very different from the savagery of Huxley's Darwinism.

Biologists such as David Sloan Wilson and philosopher of biology Elliot Sober think evolution doesn't worry about passing on individual copies of any given parent. They think evolution is worried about ensuring the survival of the species—species that are somewhat altruistic in nature—even to the point of sacrificing individual lives so others may live. So, do you think the answer to the question "Why *be* moral?" is simply that it is built into the genes of our species? Explain your thinking.

Some economists and biologists along with some linguists believe that the moral language we evolved, along with our moral practices with regard to one another, bespeaks a very mysterious phenomenon about our species. We have no evidence that any other species worries about matters of morality, so why do you suppose it has become an issue for human beings?

We have no evidence that the language fragments some other species have employed for signaling to one another lead such species to moral reflection. Humans use moral reasoning to influence each other. And humans privately deliberate on matters of morality hoping to ensure their own subsequent behavior is somehow right-minded. Why do humans care at all about such things? Why should our private moral deliberations matter so much to us? Why do you suppose humans created a language that made private moral reflection possible?

St. Thomas Aquinas thinks that through reason one can find in nature the basis of the morality that God intended. If humans by nature are destined to reflect on matters of morality, it is because God built that into human nature. Moral truth, while not always easy to identify, is something that can be gotten at through extensive reasoning about the natural organization of human beings. Without God there would be no force behind moral reason. What do you think?

Plato believed in no god. Yet Plato did believe that there were ideal forms of how this imperfect world ought to be. Among those ideal forms for Plato were things like truth, beauty, and justice. Only the ignorant fail to bring their behavior into accord with the ultimately beautiful, true, and just. Is this an adequate response to the question "Why should we be moral?"

Finally, G. E. Moore says we just have a natural intuition for the morally good and an aversion to the morally bad. His answer to the question "Why should we be moral?" would presumably be something like, "What reason could there possibly be for wanting to be any other way?" Do you think this interpretation of Moore is at all helpful in understanding the initial claim with which we began, "Why be moral?" Explain.

John Nash talks about securing a mathematical equilibrium wherein no one loses but all might gain differential amounts. He thinks mathematical game theory allows us to get rid of emotions and solve all moral problems with mathematical rigor once we have mathematized all inputs. Do you think all inputs to a decision challenge can be mathematized? Do you think this is a way to move us away from a debased morality of the crowds to a higher morality honoring the species as a whole?

So, why be moral?

# Appendix A: Resources for Further Information

## WEBSITE AT SAM HOUSTON STATE UNIVERSITY

You now have a good start developing critical thinking in your students as your mandated curriculum may allow. Your supply of scripts may well fill up a year. Then again, maybe not. In case you have a need for further scripts, we outlined in Appendix B the protocol for writing your own scripts.

Some teachers may not want to write their own scripts, or they may be unsure if a script they are writing models the scripts contained herein sufficiently to be effective. Rather than abandon the teacher to make or break it on his or her own, we intend to stand by and assist you as much as we can and as much as you may wish. To do this, we have established a website at Sam Houston State University (SHSU) to continue to assist you as your time and needs evolve.

The website will serve several purposes. First, you may submit questions about script content and discussion structure or request review of a script you have prepared on your own. You can expect a return from us in four business days while school is in session each year. Second, from time to time we post a new script on the website that will be freely available to all users of the system.

Third, if a school or district decides it would like a workshop or even a yearlong piloted program in their district, they can contact the website to request one or more of the authors to respond and manage the request in detail. Finally, there are a number of programs around the world that develop communities of inquiry for students in one way or another. The website will maintain a clearinghouse of such programs to the extent that we know about them. The address of the website is: thinkingbeyondthetest.weebly.com. For additional information, the phone number to contact Daphne D. Johnson at Sam Houston is (936) 294-3875.

## BOOKS ON ENGAGING STUDENTS IN COMMUNITIES OF INQUIRY

*Thinking Through Philosophy* Books 1, 2, 3, and 4 (2002) by Paul Cleghorn and Stephanie Baudet. Each book in the series features a number of stories, mysteries, and other discussion starters and a step-by-step process for creating and maintaining a community of inquiry in the classroom.

*Argue with Me* (second edition, 2016) by Deanna Kuhn, Laura Hemberger, and Valerie Khait is available from Routledge. This book is based on Deanna Kuhn's highly regarded, decades-long research study of argumentation skills, and it is a handbook intended to aid the classroom teacher.

*The Philosophical Child* (2012) by Jana Mohr Lone and *Philosophy in Education* (2016) by Jana Mohr Lone and Michael D. Burroughs. Both books are available from Rowman & Littlefield. The earlier book gives an introduction to structuring dialogues in the classroom on open-ended topics, while the second mostly furnishes a set of materials for classroom use.

*Big Ideas for Little Kids* (2009) by Thomas Wartenberg is also available from Rowman & Littlefield. It uses children's literature, for example *The Giving Tree*, to lead students into discussing philosophical ideas.

Finally, an older book from Temple University Press, *Philosophy in the Classroom* (1980, second edition) by Matthew Lipman, AnnMargaret Sharp, and Frederick Oscanyan, gives the interested reader an overview of topics such as "Encouraging Children to Be Thoughtful" and "Applying Thinking Skills to School Experience."

## INSTITUTIONS THAT SUPPORT PROGRAMS TO INVOLVE STUDENTS IN THE GREAT CONVERSATION

The University of Hawaii at Manoa Uehiro Academy for Philosophy and Education at http://p4chawaii.org. This program has been ongoing for a number of years, and you can find all sorts of resources from a link on their homepage. One of the important things this program stresses is how structured discussions of serious questions in the school classroom contribute to cross-cultural understanding.

Under the direction of the founder, Jana Mohr Lone, the University of Washington's Center for Philosophy for Children is affiliated with the University of Washington's Philosophy Department. The Center's website is at http://depts.washington.edu/nwcenter/. It gives one access to a great deal of useful information; for example, a video of a classroom discussion: https://www.youtube.com/watch?v=KfxgjFyBnAQ. The site also includes a set of model lesson plans and links to a number of helpful websites, including, for example, a program at the University of Texas El Paso, Philosophy for Children in the Borderlands.

Project Zero at Harvard University has been notable for the work of many scholars, one of the most relevant being David Perkins. Perkins is the author of books such as *Making Learning Whole: How Seven Principles of Teaching Can Transform Education.* The website for Project Zero is at www.pz.harvard.edu

In 1974 at Montclair State University the Institute for the Advancement of Philosophy for Children (IAPC) was founded with Matthew Lipman as the leading light. Since that time, the IAPC has published a number of books relating to Philosophy for Children (P4C), and has sponsored conferences, journals, and research on Philosophy for Children. For information on current activities, including an IAPC Summer Seminar, contact Joe Oyler at oylerj@mail.montclair.edu and visit the website at www.montclair.edu/cehs/academics/centers-and-institutes/iapc/

SAPERE is a British group that supports Philosophy for Children, and their website at http://www.sapere.org.uk gives anyone interested a chance to see what this can look like in the classroom. Also, SAPERE partnered with the Education Endowment Foundation to sponsor a major study of how dialogues on concepts such as truth and fairness would affect the achievement levels of students in years four and five. According to the Durham University group who evaluated the study, the program had a positive impact on students' reading and math, and this effect was biggest for disadvantaged students. See the report: https://v1.educationendowmentfoundation.org.uk/uploads/pdf/Philosophy_for_Children.pdf

A website that features materials inspired by Richard Paul is at http://www.criticalthinking.org (for a sample of this approach see a handy source, *Learning to Think Things Through: A Guide to Critical Thinking Across the Curriculum* by Gerald Nosich [fourth edition, 2011]).

Finally, for a number of video clips that show P4C in action in school classrooms, see http://www.sapere.org.uk/default.aspx?tabid=189. A website that is a bit off the beaten track but offers an approach to critical thinking involving dialogue as an essential component of critical thinking is available at http://www.cog-tech.com.

## RESOURCES FOR CRITICAL THINKING THEORY, PEDAGOGY, AND PRACTICE

There are a number of textbooks that convey an overall sense of what can be involved in the effort to teach critical-thinking principles and practices. A couple of the standard texts are *Critical Thinking: Consider the Verdict* by Bruce Waller (sixth edition, 2012) and *The Power of Critical Thinking* by Lewis Vaughn (fifth edition, 2015). Two innovative books in this area are *Reason in the Balance* by Sharon Bailin and Mark Battersby (second edition, 2016) and *THINK Critically* by Peter Facione and Carol Gittens (second edition, 2013).

In addition to Daniel Kahneman's book *Thinking, Fast and Slow* (2011), there are several books by psychologists that should be of interest to anyone concerned with critical thinking, books such as *Mindware: Tools for Smart Thinking* by Richard Nisbett (2015), *What Intelligence Tests Miss: The Psychology of Rational Thought* by Keith Stanovich (2010), and the classic *How We Know What Isn't So* by Tom Gilovich. See *Risk Savvy: How to Make Good Decisions* (2014) by Gerd Gigerenzer for a somewhat contrarian view. In addition, Fasko's book (2003) is a handy source, as the title indicates, for *Critical Thinking and Reasoning: Current Research, Theory, and Practice.*

Insight Assessment is a source for some of the most widely used tests to assess critical thinking skills and dispositions: http://www.insightassessment.com

## Journals

*Inquiry: Critical Thinking Across the Disciplines*, Sam Houston State University, three issues annually (print and online versions). *Inquiry* is a forum for the discussion of issues related to the theory, practice, and pedagogy of critical thinking across the disciplines, from precollege to university settings. The goal is to encourage an exchange of ideas about effective pedagogy in critical-thinking instruction, about methods of assessing critical-thinking skills and dispositions, about systematic errors in our thinking, about enhancing the quality of information on which we base decisions and inferences, about common fallacies in argumentation, and about all other topics that are relevant to critical thinking across the disciplines.

*Informal Logic*, University of Windsor, Canada, quarterly (online version). *Informal Logic* is a peer-reviewed journal publishing articles and reviews on topics related to reasoning and argumentation in theory and practice. It is deliberately multidisciplinary, welcoming theoretical and empirical research from any pertinent field, including, but not restricted to, philosophy, rhetoric, communication, linguistics, psychology, artificial intelligence, education, and law.

*Thinking & Reasoning*, Routledge, quarterly (print and online versions). *Thinking & Reasoning* is dedicated to the understanding of human thought processes, with particular emphasis on studies on reasoning, decision making, and problem solving. While the primary focus is on psychological studies of thinking, contributions are welcome from philosophers, artificial intelligence researchers, and other cognitive scientists whose work bears upon the central concerns of the journal. Topics published in the journal include studies of deductive reasoning, inductive reasoning, judgments of probability and other quantities, conceptual thinking, the neuropsychology of reasoning, and the influence of language and culture on thought.

*Thinking Skills and Creativity*, Elsevier, quarterly (print and online versions). *Thinking Skills and Creativity* is a journal providing a peer-reviewed forum for communication and debate for the community of researchers interested in teaching for thinking and creativity. Papers may represent a variety of theoretical perspectives and methodological approaches and may relate to any age level in a diversity of settings: formal and informal, education and work based.

# Appendix B: Building Your Own Scripts

In describing how to build your own scripts, we risk trivializing your understanding of the process. The description will make building a script sound much easier than it in fact is.

One must begin with a strong and broad-based educational background. In addition, one must be very alert when collecting practical experience. A competent script builder should always be summing and revising his or her sense of the world in which we all live (Lynch, 2005, 2016).

In sympathy with this point, British philosopher and pioneer in logic and democratic theory, John Stuart Mill, once declared that it is better to be Socrates dissatisfied than a pig satisfied. Mill meant that thinking should aim for understanding and not hedonistic satisfaction. When building scripts the task is to tantalize and challenge students to relentlessly seek better understanding and shared explanation. The task is not to say things one likes or wants to be true. The task is to pave the way toward independent and shared ventures in truth seeking for each and every discussion participant.

At the beginning of every disciplinary study there is a need for some ritualized sharing of signaling, as Robin Wiley describes it in his book *Noise Matters* (2015). From learning the alphabet and how to count and do quadratic equations there is a need to be told or shown how to do something until the student gets it right. When learning anything there is a threshold at which novices have learned enough to engage further material reflectively. This threshold leads to more reflective exercise about recognizing when students have the patience and skill to pursue a line of questioning relentlessly.

Scripts entice students to ask two questions over and again. The first question that permeates all scripting exercises is: "How do you know?" The second question is: "What do you or I mean by the term $X$?" Most scripts also require a willingness to "finish" a script with an open-ended question, somewhat rehearsing where the script began.

Plato's advice to acquire knowledge and experience before more serious thinking is sound. Take your time and always consider revising a script after you have field tested it with a class. When you find something that works, you will want to write it out in context lest you lose the valuable twists and turns you have carefully sculpted when engaging students in more freelancing, less disciplined inquiry.

## PICKING A TOPIC

*Step one*: Pick a topic that excites you. Your interest and intrigue are likely to be infectious to your students.

Caveat: your topic, while exciting to you, must also fit into the subject matter that the students are studying. This does not mean that the topic must be rubric fashioned to anticipate test items on a standardized test. Rather, it simply advises judicious discernment when selecting a topic relevant to what students are studying and are prepared to draw upon as a result of their previous learning.

## FOCUS

*Step two*: Once you have a topic in mind, narrow your focus. The great twentieth-century philosopher Ludwig Wittgenstein thought that language could often obfuscate rather than clarify an issue people want to understand more clearly. Define your terms. Both Socrates and Plato often give the impression that deeper understanding can be fleshed out simply by agreeing on the real meaning of essential terms. To sharpen focus, it is often advantageous to single out one or two terms as central to the inquiry you have in mind. For example, if you want to explore the idea of reasonableness you might start by focusing attention on the word *reason*.

## KICK OFF

*Step three*: Once you have focused on one or two terms, it is time to think about how to start a script. Usually, it is best to begin a script by asking a question about the meaning of one or two key words you have in mind. For example, if you are talking about reasonableness you might begin by simply asking the open-ended question, "What is a reason?" This is the way people enter into real conversations with one another, is it not?

Each of the scripts in this book has a title. The title is there solely for the purpose of indexing, and distinguishing the content of one script from another. Never start a scripted discussion by announcing to students the title of the script. When you begin by announcing a title you immediately move the discussion away from a genuine conversation to merely that of another classroom exercise. In the world outside of classrooms, people do not begin conversations by announcing a title for a topic they want to discuss. In the world outside of the classroom, when a person wants to initiate a discussion he or she usually starts by asking a question.

*Step four*: In many ordinary discussions the leading question is too often long winded and contains a hint of the answer the speaker wants to solicit. This is not how the leading question of a scripted discussion is to begin. In a scripted discussion the leading question should be brief and open ended. This gives wary participants a chance to get their feet wet before stepping into full-scale reflective analysis and discussion with one another.

## FOLLOW UP

*Step five*: Following the first question, there are usually further questions prompting participants more deeply into disciplined conversation. These follow-up questions are intended to lure the students into an early consensus on how to think about the matter at hand. There may also be an early exposition of a noncontentious example. The point at this early stage is to draw the students into a false sense of security that "we got this!"

The great psychologist Leon Festinger (1957) showed that when students commit to the truth of something and then find that truth is in peril they are generally more eager to engage in discussion to relieve the cognitive dissonance they feel. In the vernacular, we may say simply that when participants in the impending discussion feel they "have a dog in the race" they pay more attention to every turn.

In step five questions are designed to move forward from an open-ended challenge to clarification of a concept discussants too readily assumed was uncontroversial. The original, tentatively held consensus gives everyone a dog in the race. Once off the starting line, however, it becomes evident to participants that all dogs in the race are not lined up in uniform fashion. Differences of opinion and irregularities of competing arguments are then set forward to engage the most serious thinking of all.

## CRITICAL REVIEW

*Step six*: Create grounds for critical review. Most typically this can be accomplished by creating a scenario that seems on the surface, at least, to run counter to the previous consensus. For example, if students seemed generally agreed that a *reason* is something that causes action, the scenario offered might show how a reason may *cause* a change of belief in someone. Students should then question whether or not a *change in belief* necessarily leads to immediate change in subsequent action.

Extending the current example about reason, the script may share an illustrative story with students. For example, telling students about the mathematician Georg Cantor may prove revealing. Cantor wrestled with the idea that even though the set of odd natural numbers and natural numbers are both infinite in size, somehow the natural numbers seem as if they should in some sense count as a larger set. However one goes about resolving this apparent paradox, the reason for any decision may result in no physical action. There may be a change of belief in students' minds, but nothing more at the moment.

The purpose of the Cantor story would be to illustrate to students something unexpected and thereby create something of an "Aha" moment, showing them that things may not be as simple as they appear to be on the surface. Should all go well then participants in the discussion have an additional angle on the idea of reason that they may have previously never considered.

Note that the idea that reason animates actions has not been discarded in this scenario. Some students may argue that *actions of the mind* are like other *actions in the physical world*. The challenge then is to prompt these students to give an account justifying that possibility by asking either "What do you mean by *action*?" or "How do you *know* they are alike?" This invites students to give *plausible* reasons for hanging on to their initial intuitions. Other students who abandoned their initial intuitions about differential sizes of infinite sets should similarly be asked to explain their reasons for their revised convictions regarding infinite sets. Subsequently, all students should be asked whether or not their convictions about such matters are likely to lead to any changes in their subsequent actions in the future.

*Step seven*: At this point students are fully engaged in critical review of a concept. What do reasons do? What are reasons for? How do we know when we come across a reason? What is the connection between reasons and conclusions? What is the role of reasons in directing actions? What is the role of reasons in "being reasonable"?

At this point the scriptor should pose questions in a logical sequence that slows students from jumping to conclusions. Here the scriptor's questions following the counterexample scenario reveal to participants what it means to reflectively turn a thought over in one's mind. That reflection is what the educational philosophers John Dewey and Matthew Lipman so often encouraged. This is the heart of the script. It is here that the scriptor's talent is most prominently exhibited. Students should feel that they are engaged in a discussion that matters. They are seeking right as opposed to wrong, truth as opposed to falsehood, meaningfulness as opposed to nonsense, utility as opposed to mere fancy.

All too often discussions in classrooms degenerate into a "hide and seek" format or to a "whatever" format. In the "hide and seek" format, students quickly catch on that the only point to the discussion is to get to the answer the teacher had in mind all along. When students feel that this is what is going on it turns the discussion into little more than a simple game like Twenty Questions. In the "whatever" format, the teacher announces that in the discussion we are about to have there are no right or wrong answers! Truly? If that is the case then why have the discussion at all? Isn't this what wasting time is all about? For a discussion to matter, students must sense it can be purposeful (Sher, 2016).

For discussions to be purposeful they must at least hold promise of leading participants some distance away from errant and misguided conclusions. Guaranteeing truth does not need to be part of the deal. But progress away from error must always hold some promise of progress.

If students believe that there is no right or wrong answer to their discussion then they are likely either to trivialize the exercise in their mind or to see it as little more than a competition to win their way over classmates (Gardner, 2011). The value of discussion gets lost from the outset in the "no true or false/no right or wrong" or "whatever" announcement.

Most scripted discussions are intended to avoid identifying any position as T-R-U-T-H. On the other hand, it is very important for students to figure out that while they may not be able to identify grand cosmic truth in any sense, their shared investigation can lead them away from many errors.

Leading away from likely errors is what makes such discussion so pragmatically attractive (Wittgenstein, 1953). The idea that students can figure out a way to free themselves from at least some errors in thinking through shared discussion makes the value of critical review invaluable. When discussions are set from the outset to lead nowhere, the discussions are unproductive. At the very least, every scripted discussion should embody at least the hope for students that, as a result of the discussion, they might understand matters better and that where diversity of position continues to exist, the best reasons available for competing positions have been made evident.

## CONCLUSION

Scripting the conclusion challenges a scriptor's ego! Remember that as a scriptor you chose a topic that excited you. Yet as a scriptor you are duty bound, pedagogically speaking, to stick to the script and not enter into the students' discussion to sell or even share your own ideas.

Throughout the heart of the script, the scriptor has placed mental "landmines" (counterexamples, and questions that challenge overgeneralizations) forcing participants to dig ever deeper to justify their emerging positions.

The "wrong position," at least in the scriptor's mind, may be emerging as the apparent heir to truth in most participants' minds. The temptation to engage the students off script to "right" the apparent wrong is powerful, but the scriptor needs to resist the temptation. What matters in the end is that *any position held* by a majority, or, a minority, is held with substantial evidence or argument, weighted in its favor.

*Step eight*: One of the best ways to finish a script is to ask a question about the concept central to the discussion all over again. This may even be a repeat of the question with which the scriptor started. In the example discussing reason, the first and last question may be simply: What do we mean by the term *reason*?

## FINAL CONSIDERATIONS

The major steps to creating a script have been described. However, as the saying goes, "The devil is in the details." To address the details we now talk about: appropriate language, length, relevant examples, paragraphing, and a tactic we call "sneaking in scholars' names."

*Appropriate language*: The first thing to keep in mind is that scripts are intended to lead conversation, not to manage them. The difference between leading and managing a conversation is much the same as the difference between leading and managing in any human collective endeavor. *Leading* is a matter of getting folks to embrace their own decision-making capacities. It means getting participants to follow a discussion because it is engaging in ways that matter. In contrast, when *managing* a discussion one employs manipulative strategies to ensure the discussion goes in just the direction the manager intends.

Managers feel responsible for getting everyone to a previously dictated destination. In contrast, leaders lead by keeping a general shared focus before the mind of all participants. Leading a discussion means making it appealing to follow, generally, a path that leads to a satisfactory conclusion(s). Think about it. When teachers use scripts the purpose is to inspire and share, not manage and direct.

Language, as well as social role, greatly affects which ambience is present. When teachers use scripts they cannot avoid the fact that they are teachers. But teachers can be leaders as much as managers.

A teacher can sit down with a group of students after school and just talk. During these sit-down talks the teacher talks in his or her own voice without trying to talk down to the students in a language she or he thinks students might be able to get. Of course, the teacher doesn't use "high-falootin'" language that will go over their heads. Neither does she or he calculate what she or he thinks they are allegedly competent to understand. In addition, during such sit-down talks the teacher listens and questions the students about what they might not understand. The point here is that the language used in a script should sound like a sit-down talk. The language should capture the scriptor's natural way of speaking.

If the teacher uses a word the students are unfamiliar with, chances are they will naturally come to understand the new word in context. This has always been the most natural way children expand their vocabulary. If the student doesn't understand a word, if the ambience is a trusting one, she or he will ask, "What does X mean?" When writing a script the language should also have a bit of "folksiness" in it. By this we mean that people sharing in the discussion should get the feel that this is a genuine but casual search for some sort of shared understanding.

Managers and teachers teaching a lesson have a tendency to drive points home rather than take the more circuitous route of luring participants into figuring things out. Except for the counterexample leading into the heart of the script, language should be precise and yet always maintain an element of tentativeness in it. For example, a script should contain questions like "Do you think reasons can ever be a cause of some action?" and statements like, "There are some who think that reasons may exist but they don't cause anything to happen." In contrast, a managed discussion will simply tell them what the manager believes is true about such things.

If it is natural for the scriptor to say the word *cognitive*, the scriptor should go ahead and use it. Using that word is natural for the scriptor, and the participants at nearly any age will figure it out. For example, with ten-year-olds, if the script has a sentence such as "Are reasons just a *cognitive event* or do they involve emotions sometimes too?" most ten-year-olds probably are not familiar with the word *cognitive*. Some will figure it out right away from context. Others will figure it out after being a part of a community of peers who begin to use the word naturally in their chat with the script-using teacher. Finally, if any participants are left who have not caught on to the meaning of the word, then sooner or later they are likely to ask, "What does *cognitive* mean?"

Certainly scriptors should not use words like *ratiocination*. Can you even imagine anyone having a sit down for a discussion with nine-year-olds after school and naturally whipping out a sentence like, "Are conclusions always dependent upon ratiocination?"

The bottom line is when building a script, use language reflective of how you speak naturally in conversation. Sentences should *sound right* and not *read right*. A script is not an essay. It is a script meant to sustain animation throughout a conversation. Don't be afraid to use a colloquialism. Don't be afraid to use a cutesy folkism. For example, in discussing the difference between good reasons and bad reasons you might ask: "President Obama once said, 'You can put lipstick on a pig but it is still a pig.' Does that mean that even good reasons can't make a bad idea anything other than a bad idea?"

Colorful examples and analogies invigorate sit-down discussions and can do so when properly employed in a script as well. When a script succeeds, it produces a moment of the Great Conversation.

*Length*: Scripts for younger elementary school students should always be kept short, no more than a page and a half at most. Even though you are not dictating information to be embraced by the student's long-term memory, the limited attention span of young adolescents will make even the most cleverly constructed script a tedious task when the discussion lasts beyond thirty minutes. Scripts that create fifteen-to-twenty-minute discussions are likely to be most effective.

As students mature, they can sustain their interest in a discussion for a longer time. However, that doesn't mean that effective scripts for older students need to be longer. What it means is that as students mature, scripts of varying lengths can be effectively employed. Longer scripts for older students may contain more than one counterexample or even a description of a situation contrived to set up further discussion. Keep in mind that the purpose of the script isn't to impart information into students' minds. The purpose of the scripts is to learn more effective use of ideas the student is already somewhat familiar with.

*Relevant examples*: As noted immediately above, the purpose of the scripts is to prompt the student to use more effectively ideas she may already have in place. Examples in the script are not meant to teach participants in the discussion new textual material for assimilation, as Piaget describes most didactic instruction. The counterexamples may well extend each participant's zone of proximal development, as Vygotsky (1979) would put it, by inducing them to employ ideas in heretofore previously unconsidered ways, but even that is a secondary benefit.

First and foremost, examples are intended to inform the student of a new wrinkle to consider in regard to the matter at hand, or most often to create productive cognitive dissonance following conclusions that seem somewhat consensual among participants up to that point. For the example to be effective they must either call upon experiences likely to be well-entrenched in most participants' previous personal experience or they must be enticingly provocative to hold participant interest, as gasps of "Really?!" slip quietly through their mind as the new bit of information or exotic scenario does the job of piquing participant imagination.

*Paragraphing*: The more mature the students the more novel or extensive the presentation of new information or an extended scenario may be. The less mature students need information delivered with optimal brevity and immediate employment evident in the unfolding of a scenario or a series of questions. Less mature students also need to be primed with truncated scenarios that prompt discussion or flow into an inviting question in no more than sixty to ninety seconds.

Always keep the principle of familiarity in mind. If characters are named in the scenario, try to use proper names that sound familiar to students in the locale wherein your scripts are to be used. Again, the reason is to make entry into the discussion a welcome and familiar event, an interesting chat students might have with a slightly more worldly and sophisticated friend. Names that sound exotic, just as scenarios that seem too far-fetched given the experience of the less mature students, become distracting and an impediment to their readily engaging in the discussion.

*Sneaking in names of scholars*: Think of this as a tolerable luxury. We have already made clear that language and additional information in scenarios should adhere to a *principle of familiarity*. The principle of familiarity states simply that scripted discussions should begin well within participants' collective zone of proximal development. Scripts are for developing reasoning skills and are not to be employed for purposes of test preparation or any other kind of memorization exercise. What students are to retain from participation in scripted discussions is greater skill of reasoning.

There is a difference between *knowing that* and *knowing how* (Ryle, 1949). For example, we *know that* there are four authors of this book. *Knowing that* fact tells the reader nothing about *knowing how* to read this book in order to extract from it as much meaning as possible. This book is about developing further *know how* in students. It is not a book cataloguing facts for drill and grill. This means that adhering to the principle of familiarity is critical for ensuring that students feel welcomed into participation rather than challenged to grasp new facts. Will the students learn new facts and ideas despite that not being an objective of the script? Ask them.

When you ask students if they learned from their participation in the scripted discussion you will learn three things if the script was successfully constructed. First, you will learn that the students believe they learned a great deal about their own thinking in the matter. Second, students will report that they learned the ideas explored were much more involved than they initially expected. Third, they will report that they learned important things from one another and not just from the scriptor downloading information. When students report awareness of their learning these things, you will have confirmation that you brought the students into a moment of the Great Conversation of Humankind.

Paying attention to the *Principle of Familiarity* does not preclude using some language that may not be generally familiar to all student participants. As noted above, if the unfamiliar language captures the manner in which the scriptor would normally have a sit-down chat with students on the schoolhouse steps after school, the students will probably catch on to the term in context.

In addition, in the ambience of a sit-down chat, participants are likely to feel comfortable asking for clarification of any word they do not understand. The Principle of Familiarity is a strongly intended heuristic when building a script. Sometimes the scriptor may so love a certain author that she or he wants to build the author's name into a script. On occasion that is perfectly all right. However, the scriptor must not give into the temptation of ever testing students over the name of anyone mentioned in a script lest the script deteriorate into nothing other than an exercise in Piagetian assimilation.

For example, we may find ourselves drawn to want to share with the reader now that many writers have made allusion to the distinction between *knowing how* and *knowing that*. The first one to do so using those exact words was the legendary twentieth-century philosopher Gilbert Ryle (1949). That tidbit of information adds nothing to what we are discussing here or anywhere else in this book.

Sometimes attributions are done to give credit where credit is due—especially in scholarly journals—but other times it may turn out to be little more than a bit of hero worship on the part of the authors. That is just fine unless digression finds its way into something readers begin to fear they will be tested over.

Sometimes the scriptor may include a scholar's name on the off chance that students might remember it and, if they do, fine. If not, again, fine. Remembering names is not what critical thinking is all about, any more than critical thinking is about coming up with teacher-approved ideas.

So, for example, in building a script on morality, a scriptor might write, "There was a Greek philosopher once long ago who thought it is impossible to figure out all the right things to do in each and every case. This guy, named Aristotle, thought the best we can do is look at our intentions to figure out if we are acting virtuously. What do you think? Is figuring out our intentions important to figuring out whether what we are doing is good or bad, right or wrong, or even just OK?"

Notice, Aristotle's name is slipped in conversationally. Some participants may recognize it vaguely as an important name and remember it. That's an incidental bonus in this process. Others may forget the name almost immediately and focus in on the idea of intentions or virtues. That too is just fine. If the student picks up a passing acquaintance with a great intellect that might lead to some greater interest one day, that is fine. However, such learning is always incidental to the process scripts focus on. The incidental should never distract participants from learning from the core process.

Educational psychology tells us incidental learning has a tendency to dominate classroom activity. Your script, focusing as it does on process rather than product, should naturally align itself with much of what is normally considered incidental. And if some participants incidentally remember that Aristotle was one of the architects of Western philosophy, that bit of "knowing that" is a bonus rather than an interference with the "learning how" to think critically that is the focus of instruction.

There is one other reason for slipping in a name. If the script builder is crafting a script for a particular lesson, bringing in a name the students are familiar with may provide some contextual familiarity. A script developed for a particular subject may also be a way to introduce a figure central to some studies ahead without making it a centerpiece of some didactic instruction aimed at some standardized test ahead. So a history teacher may find using the name Aristotle beneficial in context, as a science teacher might find Mendelev worth mentioning if instruction in the periodic table is part of the curriculum, and so on.

## THE SCRIPT YOU BUILD WILL BE YOUR OWN

There is an upside and a downside to this rather obvious fact. The upside is that in building a script you are investing in a discussion you are already excited about and likely to share affection for when introducing the script to students. The downside is that it is very difficult not to sell your ideas, leveraging your authority as teacher or scriptor to ensure the production of consensus you favor (Zagzebski, 2012). Your task is to draw on your experience, research, and other learning to lead participants into a discussion. You must muster the courage to trust your students that the path they variously finish is not interfered with by your desire to see the world strictly as you do.

In Appendix C we introduce you to some background considerations in logic and statistical inference. It would be easy for you to read that as some facts students should know. When teachers come across "facts the student should know" there is often an irresistible temptation to test over the facts to show some accountability. Do not give into that temptation in this case!

Appendix C is essentially a primer in the use of a handful of words and the patterns they display when competently used. *This is a primer for you, the teacher*. It is not a primer for students. It is not subject matter to test students over.

The key words in Appendix C are little words. They are little words that are key to moving around and evaluating chunks of thought. These words, such as *If → Then, therefore, probably, so, not, hence, because*, and others, are words known as *logical operators*. Logical operators move chunks of thought about in systematic ways for review and critique when well executed.

Knowing more about the expert use of logical operators will help give you, the teacher, better skill at explanation to students throughout the curriculum. This general role-modeling to students is invaluable and will help them gain more from scripted discussions eventually. The reason you, the teacher, should learn more skillful employment of those words and the accompanying inference patterns they imply is that it will put you in a better position to evaluate how well the students' intuitional grasp of those operators is improving over the year as they become more accustomed to the comfort of scripted discussions.

In short, your developing familiarity with logical operators is another product of attending to the principle of familiarity generally. Your ease and acquaintance with the comfortable and proper use of the logical operators in standard classroom conversation will slide into those comfortable sit-down conversations we mentioned above.

Scripted discussions prompt student attention to logical operators and semantic accuracy without formal instruction. Consequently, logical thinking becomes more natural as it simply becomes a familiar piece of classroom discussion ambience. You are there to lead. Leaders lead best when they have a vision of destiny.

# Appendix C: Elements of Mindware

*Mindware* is a handy term. It denotes "tools for smart thinking," as in the title of Richard Nisbett's book by that name (Nisbett, 2015). There are many mindware tools, and to address them all would require a book like Nisbett wrote. Also, some of the tools are highly sophisticated, and explaining them can take a book by itself. In this Appendix we focus only on basic elements of mindware that are relatively straightforward to grasp but have great power to keep thinking from going awry.

MINDWARE TOOLS OF DEDUCTIVE REASONING

## The Fundamental Concept: Deductive Validity

There are many uses for the term *valid*. Consider, for example, the sentence "Evelyn's suspicions about Tom are valid." It seems here the suggestion is that Evelyn knows what she is talking about. In contrast, here is a different and very special sense of the term *valid*. This second sense of valid refers not to an alleged knowledge base but rather to the reliability of a line of reasoning. Everyone is familiar with this special sense of validity, although maybe not with the specific terminology in mind. Consider this line of reasoning:

Tom is taller that Dick and
<u>Dick is taller than Harry, so therefore</u>
Tom is taller than Harry.

You don't know Tom, Dick, and Harry, but you understand that **if** statements one and two are true, **then** statement three *has to be* true. The "has to be true" relationship means that the truth of the conclusion is necessarily true **if** the premises (the starting points of the reasoning) are true. The "has to be true relationship" is what *deductive* validity is about. Of course, when thinking about how the world is, there is no absolute guarantee of the T-R-U-T-H. This is because, even when using deductively valid reasoning, if one or more of the premises is false the truth value of the conclusion is at risk. Remember the old computer tech warning: "Garbage in, garbage out." Nonetheless, deductive reasoning is one of the most important pieces of mindware needed when engaging in serious thought and discussion with others.

Surprisingly, you may discover, if you haven't already, that learning to reason is crucially dependent on learning to use certain small words skillfully! These small words include some of the most often-used words in both your and your students' vocabularies. The words include: *if*, *then*, *so*, *because*, *therefore*, *hence*, *not*, *and*, *or*, *but*, *consequently*—among others. But as you may or certainly will notice shortly, there is a big difference between learning to use these words and learning to use them appropriately as one executes a piece of reasoning.

## Iffy Connections

Hypothetical reasoning with **if** (and other words with similar meanings) is something we commonly do. Sometimes we do it well, and, sometimes, we do it not so well. Learning to do it well is another mindware tool. For example, it is a good bet we are reasoning when we reason along the following lines:

> **If** Tom passes the final exam, **then** Tom will pass the course.
> Tom just got his exam back with a passing grade on it, so
> Tom will pass the course.

Neither of the first two statements is assumed or guaranteed to be true by itself, but **if** both of the statements are true, **then** the last statement must be true as well. This piece of reasoning fits a pattern that is pretty evident:

> **If** A, **then** B is true and
> A is true, therefore
> B is true.

Call this pattern of valid reasoning Affirming the Antecedent. Statement A is *the antecedent* in the "If → Then" reasoning above; that is, statement 1, and the other premise, statement 2, affirms that A is true. So, begin with the assumption that A leads to B and add to that the assumption that A is true, we can reliably conclude that **therefore** B is true.

*Elements of Mindware* 91

Consider a second deductive pattern in our mindware toolkit:

**If** it rained last night, **then** the driveway will be wet this morning, **but**
The driveway is not wet, so therefore
It did **not** rain last night.

You can see that there is a pattern here as well, one that looks like this:

**If** the hypothesis H is true, **then** the prediction P is true, **but**
P is false, therefore
H is false.

This pattern is deductively valid, which means that the truth of the two premises guarantees the truth of the conclusion that H is false. Call this pattern Denying the Consequent. The *consequent* is the back part of an "If →Then" statement; that is, the prediction P and the second premise says that P is false and so denies that the consequent is correct.

To see what the significance is of differentiating between these two patterns of "If → Then" reasoning, contrast two similar-sounding examples involving a medical diagnostic hypothesis. The hypothesis H is that Ralph has malaria. To *test* that hypothesis, we need to make a prediction P about something we can observe that will confirm or disconfirm the truth of H. Suppose that, if Ralph has malaria (H), the prediction is that we will observe a pattern of recurring fever (P). If after keeping track of Ralph's temperature and finding no pattern of recurring fever, the prediction P is false.

Presumably this shows the hypothesis H being tested is false; in other words, Ralph does *not* have malaria. Our observation, namely that the prediction P made by the hypothesis turned out to be false, *refutes* or *falsifies* the hypothesis H. Remember how strong this reasoning is. **If** we have correctly inferred the prediction from the hypothesis and **if** we have accurately observed that the prediction is false, **then** the hypothesis *has to be* false.

No matter how interesting the hypothesis, no matter how brilliant it seems, no matter how well it fits with previous evidence, **if** we have got the inference from the hypothesis to the prediction correct and **if** our observation that the prediction failed to confirm is correct, then we have a situation in which, as Thomas Huxley put it, we may be witnessing "the slaying of a beautiful hypothesis by an ugly fact."

But there's more. We have only considered the negative outcome where the failure of the prediction falsifies the hypothesis. What happens when we get a positive outcome? What happens when, instead of Denying the Consequent, we Affirm the Consequent? This is a third pattern, and while similar on the surface it leads to unsupportable inferences. Beware!

Return to the case of Ralph and the hypothesis that he has malaria. If he has malaria, then there will be a pattern of recurring fever. Suppose there is a confirming outcome (he has a recurring fever), then the situation looks like this:

**If** Ralph has malaria, **then** he will have a pattern of recurring fever.
Ralph does have a pattern of recurring fever, therefore
Ralph has malaria.

It does not take an expert thinker or medical specialist to understand that this is a weak piece of reasoning. First, there is the obvious background fact in common knowledge that there are many diverse causes of recurrent fevers. The observation in this third scenario does *fit with* the malaria hypothesis, but it fits just as well with hundreds of other diagnostic hypotheses. So how useful is this bit of risky reasoning? Certainly not sound enough to put this pattern into our mindware toolkit!

In general, the Affirming the Consequent pattern of reasoning involves confirming results, and it looks like this:

**If** the hypothesis H is true, **then** the prediction P is true, **and**
P is in fact true, therefore
The hypothesis H is true.

But idea buyers should beware! Even if the statements are true, they do NOT guarantee the truth of hypothesis H. The moral of the story is that confirming results, *all by themselves*, are not nearly as logically powerful as falsifying results. Take a minute before reading more. Can you explain why this fact of logic is true?

This third pattern has led some people to make an overstatement that "in science we never prove anything; the best we can do is to disprove something." While this is an exaggeration (we really have proven that the earth goes around the sun and not vice versa), it is not a substantial exaggeration. Nonetheless, the tool for the mindware kit is as follows: if we are going to *genuinely test* our ideas about how things work, we need to look, not just for evidence that fits with those ideas, but also equally hard for evidence that contradicts our favored theories and predictions.

Imagine a homicide detective early in the investigation who forms a premature hypothesis about a particular person being the murderer. That may cause him to focus only on proving his suspicion without giving serious attention to other alternatives or to exculpatory evidence. Analogously, imagine a doctor who makes a premature diagnosis and then looks only toward symptoms that confirm the doctor's initial suspicion. This pattern of faulty reasoning is called *confirmation bias*. The antidote to this bias is now in your mindware toolkit. Always be sure to look for *falsifying* evidence before endorsing a conclusion.

## MINDWARE TOOLS OF INDUCTIVE REASONING

### Sampling and Generalizing

We all must generalize in order to cope with the diversity of situations and people we encounter. (Note that generalization!) The mindware tool is: generalize carefully and efficiently. If I am going to claim, for example, that my feline leukemia vaccine works to prevent cats from dying of that disease, I ought to have evidence from a sufficiently large and random sample to back up what I am claiming.

Consider some basics. First, a generalization can be of the "all" or "none" variety, like "All of Shakespeare's plays are in blank verse" or "None of the currency in my wallet is a $100 bill." But generalizations can also take the form of percentage statements or proportions, such as "Only 8 percent of Americans have ever piloted an aircraft" or "Most Americans pay their income taxes." Any statement that characterizes a whole population of things, people, situations, or events is a *generalization*.

We cannot exhaustively observe each member of a large group. Instead, we take a sample from the population. The first question that confronts us is: How likely is it that the sample *represents* the group as a whole? There has been a great deal of thought given to these matters for over a century, and determining whether a particular sample is representative enough for one's purposes is seldom a completely straightforward matter. However, there are two factors that are fundamental: (a) the size of the sample and (b) how the members of the sample were collected.

So our second question is: How do we collect samples to increase the accuracy of their distribution matching the entire population when looked at as a whole? For example, assume Jojo has a job as an intern with the State Wildlife Department. Her job is to sample the fish population of State Lake to see what kinds of fish are there. Jojo throws a net into the lake, retrieves it, and then records the number and kinds of fish caught. She moves around the edge of the lake repeating the procedure until she has circled the entire lake. She has caught a very large sample of about 1,500 fish.

Do you see something problematic about the way Jojo gathered the fish? Tossing a net in from the bank of the lake will not collect fish from the deeper, often colder, central parts of the lake. We do not have to know much about differences between fish to suspect that some kinds of fish may prefer deeper water, and those kinds are less likely to be caught around the edge of the lake. In short, the sample was collected in a way that may *systematically overrepresent* some kinds of fish in the lake and underrepresent others. The summary percentages she attributes to the lake's population could be strongly affected by a poorly conducted plan for sampling. The name for this systematic tendency is *bias*. Be very clear that *bias* in this sense need not involve any sort of prejudice. Prejudice is a more deliberative or intentionally neglectful way of collecting and summing the results of a sampling strategy.

Consider another example: conducting a telephone survey for predicting an election outcome. If one relies on telephone landlines, thereby not using the harder-to-get cell phone numbers of a population, then it is like casting one's sampling net into the edges of the lake only. The people who have landlines may represent an older, more settled population than those who rely on cell phones alone. If that is true, then the survey runs the risk of overrepresenting older people.

The antidote for bias is to secure the most *random* sample possible. When asking whether a generalization is warranted, ask what biases may have infected the sampling process and how much those biases matter. For example, think again about the political opinion survey that disproportionately leaves out younger people. Does this matter? What if these younger people tend not to vote? Even if they are underrepresented, it may not matter much as far as predicting the election results.

In addition to a possible bias in the sampling process, the other fundamental concern is whether the sample is large enough. No matter how careful we are in selecting a sample, if it is too small—like a sample of five Americans out of a population of over three hundred million—then there is a substantial risk that *just by bad luck* the sample will not represent the larger population from which it was drawn.

The good news for inclusion in your mindware toolkit is that a sample does *not* have to be a particular proportion of a very large population—like all Americans—to have a good chance of being representative. It is more a matter of its absolute size. A *random* sample of 1,500 people can be very representative of 300,000,000.

Typically people do not understand statistical inferences as well as they should when drawing conclusions, and they tend to overextend their generalizations from mere anecdotal evidence. An anecdote is a vivid story about a particular situation. People often tell anecdotes to support a generalization. Imagine a person who returns from a trip to Alabama. She tells a story about how she received help when her car broke down. Suppose her point in telling the story is to support the assertion that "Alabamans are generally helpful."

That statement might actually be true, but an anecdote used to support a generalization is simply *a sample of size one, selected, not randomly, but precisely because it supports the generalization.* If the generalization matters then, savvy thinkers need *a representative sample*. The sample should be large and selected as randomly as possible. Be sure to put this in your mindware toolkit.

## Correlation and Causation

A *correlation* is *a pattern in the data*. Suppose we conducted a large survey, based on a random sampling, of smoking among firefighters. Because the survey is large and is random, we are not concerned now with issues of bias and random sampling error. When we find that 40 percent of firefighters are smokers, we are confident about the results.

We do not yet have a correlation, however. We must also add the information that only 20 percent of *nonfirefighters* are smokers. With that contrast information, then we can say that a person's chance of being a smoker is twice as great if that person is a firefighter than if they are not. So, being a firefighter and being a smoker are positively correlated in our data. But correlation is NOT the same as causation.

Results like these could lead us to think that smoking is an occupational hazard of firefighters. We could hypothesize that the tempo of the job, with long stretches of boring routine punctuated by brief periods of intense activity, has the effect of making it more likely that someone smokes. In general, when *A is correlated with B*, then *one possible explanation* of the correlation is that *A causes B*. But there are other possible explanations. Each of these needs to be ruled out before the correlation in the data can be proposed as evidence for the cause-and-effect conclusion.

The usual rule when A is correlated with B is that there are four possible explanations to explain the correlation: (1) A causes B, (2) B causes A, (3) a third factor C causes A and causes B, or (4) it is a coincidence.

In the example immediately above, alternative (2) seems highly unlikely. B causing A would mean being a smoker causes someone to become a firefighter. Set this aside as highly implausible. But what should be said about option (3) C causing A and B and, option (4) coincidence?

Neither possibility has been discredited. When trying to figure out how things work in a complicated world, it can be very helpful to discover a correlation in the data. The correlation can be a *clue* to uncovering a cause-and-effect relationship. Years ago doctors noticed a correlation between smoking habits and lung cancer. This correlation raised suspicions that led to serious investigation and finally the Surgeon General's warning that smoking is dangerous to one's health.

It should be clear now why it is a mistake to leap to a conclusion that, since your data show that A is correlated with B, then A causes B. That firefighters may also disproportionately count as smokers is a clue worthy perhaps of further investigation. The correlation as it stands surely does not *all by itself* substantiate a causal relationship.

## Experiments: The "Gold Standard" of the Randomized Comparative Trial

Suppose your local vet claims to have developed a new vaccine that will prevent feline leukemia. He supports his claim by saying that he gave the vaccine to ten cats and then exposed them to the virus. Only one developed feline leukemia afterward, so he claims the vaccine was a success. But was it?

There are a number of things that are questionable about the vet's reasoning. Consider these few. The base infection rate for feline leukemia in the cat population is 2 percent or 3 percent. Cats are not especially vulnerable to feline leukemia. By using only ten cats in the experiment a zero infection rate may occur *by chance*.

Such faulty reasoning happens often when working with a sample that is too small. So the next mindware tool to put in your kit is remember when evaluating experimental data to figure out whether or not the sample size is large enough to generalize the results to the larger population from which the sample is drawn.

If the vet used a sample of one thousand instead of ten, that is better, but the next mindware tool for your kit is to ask in such situations how samples were collected. If the sample was *a convenience sample* of the first one thousand cats the vet could easily acquire, that raises the possibility of a biased sample. If the one thousand cats were all strays or of a select breed, that may shed little light on the alleged responsiveness of the cat population to the vaccine.

And there is yet more. What if it turns out that having dry, rather than damp, litter boxes helps prevent the spread of feline leukemia? In addition, there may be other factors responsible for a lower infection rate among the sample population. The term for this avoidable flaw in thinking is *confounding*. The results of a study are confounded when we cannot tell with well-grounded confidence what accounts for the observed outcomes. The mindware tool is to eliminate any plausible cause of an observation before endorsing one or more actual causal candidates.

The more the vet knows about factors that can affect the chances of a cat developing feline leukemia, the better job the vet can do to justify his claims to critical thinkers that his vaccine deserves notice and further investigation.

## MINDWARE TOOLS OF ARGUMENTATION: CLASSICAL FALLACIES

There have been a number of common fallacies identified over the centuries. You are probably familiar with many of them, but you need to know why they are faulty.

*Appeal to Authority.* This fallacy addresses situations in which a person is an expert in a field but whatever expertise the expert may or may not have is not relevant to the claim of the matter at hand. For example, Michael Jordan is quite an expert on matters pertaining to basketball, but that, however, does not carry over to making him an expert in clothing design or fabric texture.

The mindware tool here is not to confuse genuine authorities with faux authorities. Keep in mind too that people of equal and legitimate authority may at times disagree, and so the matter of plausible truth cannot be settled by going to experts who themselves do not agree with one another.

*Appeal to Traditional Wisdom.* "We've always done X (and it has worked OK), so X is the thing to do." The length of time something has worked in the past is a mark in its favor. Still, X's resilience over time cannot now be allowed to settle the matter every time. For example, conditions may have changed over time, and imaginative and novel insights sometimes produce valuable angles into a problem previously overlooked.

*Appeal to Popularity.* This is reasoning from "Everybody (or a majority, etc.) thinks that X is right" to "Therefore, X is right." This fallacy tries to support a conclusion about a policy or point of view by citing the extensive acceptance it enjoys. The difficulty with this line of reasoning is that the majority may be mistaken.

The root mistake in this fallacy is failure to pay attention to what the reasons are for why the majority thinks the way that it does.

*Appeal to Common Practice.* The reasoning in this fallacy goes like this: "Since everybody (or almost everybody) is doing X, then it is not so bad for us to do X." This sounds very similar to the *Appeal to Popularity*, but there is a difference of emphasis. The *Appeal to Common Practice* is used as a blame-deflecting device, as a way of trying to argue against criticism that one may receive. It is defensive in character, and the root of the fallacy lies in a failure to give a real reason why the questioned practice should be continued.

*Straw Man Fallacy.* The Straw Man fallacy is a kind of *misrepresentation*. What happens is that a misrepresentation of an opponent's views is put forth, and a critic fights with the misrepresented portrayal (hence, the "straw man") of his adversary's position.

*False Dilemma.* This is a *fallacy of too few alternatives*. This is not a matter of having only two alternatives, like the notion of a dilemma might suggest. What matters is whether an alternative that ought to be considered has been left out in a thinker's or group of thinkers' rush to judgment.

*Begging the Question.* The person making the argument takes for granted a premise that the intended audience doubts and then he or she treats a conclusion as substantiated by the very premise originally in doubt.

*Suppressed Evidence.* This is a fallacy of ignoring inconvenient evidence. Suppressed evidence occurs when a vital piece of evidence that bears *negatively* on an advocate's conclusion is *omitted*. To diagnose this fallacy, clearly state the conclusion being considered, and then explain how the evidence that is missing could fundamentally change the plausibility of the conclusion.

*Slippery Slope.* The person making the Slippery Slope argument is predicting that if we take the first step, we will set in motion a chain of events that will lead us *inevitably* to *disaster*. So, the conclusion of the Slippery Slope is a warning not to take the first step. The fallacy lays in the fact that one or more of the steps along the way are too weak to justify the warning.

*Ad Hominem.* This occurs when name calling is used to distract people's attention from examining the argument an opponent has put forward. Instead we are asked to look at some allegedly negative characteristic of the person. When the language used to evaluate an argument becomes a personal attack on the opponent, this discredits the critic's argument and sets him or her outside the bounds of decency and respect that is inherently central in the Great Conversation of Humankind.

*Two Wrongs Make a Right.* This is best understood as *unthinking retaliation*. The mistake is thinking that an action that is ordinarily wrong becomes right just because it is being done in response to an earlier hurt. Retaliation may well be a very sensible course of action at times, but simply citing the fact of the earlier hurt does not *all by itself* make retaliation justified.

*Questionable Analogy.* Almost any two things can be viewed as "similar" depending on the point of view that one adopts. The challenge is usually "Are the two things being compared *similar enough* so that a relevant conclusion about one can be drawn from familiarity with the other?" To critically evaluate the analogy, one should be able to cite relevant differences. The differences that are relevant are determined by reference to the conclusion, so not just any difference will do.

## YOUR PERSONAL MINDWARE TOOLKIT

We hope that you will keep these tools in your personal mindware toolkit and that you will encourage others to use them. If you would like to pursue acquiring more mindware tools and sharpening the ones you have, please consult Appendix A, our guide to further information, and our list of references for relevant items.

# References

Angrist, J., & Lavy, V. (2009). The effects of high stakes high school achievement awards: Evidence from a group-randomized trial. *American Economic Review, 99*(4), 1384–1414.

Ariely, D. (2012). *The honest truth about dishonesty*. New York: Harper Collins.

Axelrod, R., & Hamilton, W. (1981). The evolution of cooperation. *Science, 211*, 1390–96.

Barell, J. (1995). *Teaching for thoughtfulness: Classroom strategies to enhance intellectual development* (second ed.). White Plains, NY: Longman.

Bazerman, M. H., & Tenbrunsel, A. E. (2011). *Blind spots: Why we fail to do what is right and what to do about it*. Princeton, NJ: Princeton University Press.

Berwick, R., & Chomsky, N. (2016). *Why only us: Language and evolution*. Cambridge, MA: MIT Press.

Bicchieri, C. (2006). *The grammar of society: The nature and dynamics of social norms*. New York: Cambridge University Press.

Bowles, S. (2016). *The moral economy: Why good incentives are no substitute for good people*. New Haven, CT: Yale University Press.

Bowles, S., & Gintis, H. (2011). *A cooperative species: Human reciprocity and its evolution*. Princeton, NJ: Princeton University Press.

Brown, D. (2009). *The Da Vinci Code*. New York: Doubleday Anchor.

Browne, M. N., & Keeley, S. M. (2010). *Asking the right questions: A guide to critical thinking* (ninth edition). Upper Saddle River, NJ: Pearson.

Castelli, I., Massaro, D., Bicchieri, C. A., Chavez, A., & Marchetti, A. (2014). Fairness norms and theory of mind in an ultimatum game: Judgments, offers and decisions in school-aged children. *PLoS ONE 9*(8): e105024, doi:10.1371/journal.pone.0105024.

Christian, B., & Griffiths, T. (2016). *Algorithms to live by: The computer science of human decisions*. New York: Henry Holt.

de Waal, F. (2016). *Are we smart enough to know how smart animals are?* New York: Norton.

Fasko, D. (ed.). (2003). *Critical thinking and reasoning: Current theories, research, and practice*. Cresskill, NJ: Hampton

Fehr, E., & Fischbacher, U. (2003). The nature of human altruism. *Nature, 425*, 785–91.

Festinger, L. (1957). *A theory of cognitive dissonance*. Stanford, CA: Stanford University Press.

Feynman, R., & Leighton, R. (1985). *"Surely you're joking, Mr. Feynman!": Adventures of a curious character*. New York: Norton.

Gardner, H. (2011). *Truth, beauty and goodness: Educating for the virtues in the age of truthiness and Twitter*. New York: Basic Books.

Gneezy, U., & Rustichini, A. (2000). Pay enough or don't pay at all. *Quarterly Journal of Economics, 115*(3), 791–810.

Gopnik, A. (2010). How babies think. *Scientific American*, *303*(1), 76–81.
Grant, R. (2012). *Strings attached: Untangling the ethics of incentives*. Princeton, NJ: Princeton University Press.
Hacking, I. (2001). *An introduction to probability and inductive logic*. Cambridge, England: Cambridge University Press.
Hanson, N. (1958). *Patterns of discovery: An inquiry into the nature of the conceptual foundations of science*. Cambridge, England: Cambridge University Press.
Heiman, M., & Slomianko, J. (1985). *Critical thinking skills*. Washington, DC: NEA.
Herrmann, B., Thoni, C., & Gachter, S. (2008). Antisocial punishment across societies. *Science, 319*, 1362–67.
Horsten, L. (2011). *The Tarskian turn: Deflationism and axiomatic truth*. Cambridge, MA: MIT Press.
House, B., Silk, J., Henrich, J., Clark Barrett, H., Scelza, B. A. et al. (2013). Ontogeny of prosocial behavior across diverse societies. *PNAS, 110*(36), 14586–591.
Koertge, N. (1998). *A house built on sand: Exposing postmodernist myths about science*. Oxford, England: Oxford University Press.
Kuhn, T. (1970). *The structure of scientific revolutions* (second edition). Chicago, IL: University of Chicago Press.
Kuhn, T. (1987). *Black-body theory and the quantum discontinuity, 1894–1912*. Oxford, England: Oxford University Press.
Lacewing, M. (2015). Philosophy, academic philosophy, and philosophy for children. *Philosopher's Magazine, 69*(2), 90–97.
Lord, E., & Maguire, B. (2016). *Weighing reasons*. Oxford, England: Oxford University Press.
Lynch, M. P. (2005). *True to life: Why truth matters*. Cambridge, MA: MIT Press.
Lynch, M. P. (2016). *The internet of us: Knowing more and understanding less in the age of big data*. New York: Liveright.
Miles, C., & Rauton, J. (1985). *Thinking tools*. Clearwater, FL: H & H Publishing.
Miller, G. A. (1956). The magical number seven, plus or minus two: Some limits on our capacity for processing information. *Psychological Review, 63*, 81–97.
Mischel, W., Ebbesen, W. E., & Zeiss, A. (1972). Cognitive and attentional mechanisms in delay of gratification. *Journal of Personality and Social Psychology, 21*, 204–18.
Mlodinow, L. (2016). *The upright thinkers: The human journey from living in trees to understanding the cosmos*. New York: Vintage.
Moore, B. R. (2004). The evolution of learning. *Biological Review, 79*(2), 301–35.
Nisbett, R. (2015). *Mindware*. New York, NY: Farrar, Straus & Giroux.
Nowak, M., & Highfield, R. (2012). *SuperCooperators: Altruism, evolution, and why we need each other to succeed*. New York: Free Press.
Olson, K. R., & Spelke, E. S. (2008). Foundations of cooperation among young children. *Cognition, 108*, 222–31.
Perkins, D. (2010). *Making learning whole*. San Francisco, CA: Jossey-Bass.
Raeburn, P., & Zollman, K. (2016). *The game theorist's guide to parenting*. New York: Scientific American.
Ryle, G. (1949). *The concept of mind*. New York: Barnes & Noble.
Sher, G. (2016). *Epistemic friction: An essay on knowledge, truth and logic*. Oxford, England: Oxford University Press.
Simon, H. (1980). *Models of thought*. New Haven, CT: Yale University Press.
Simon, H. (1984). *Models of bounded rationality, vol. 1*. Cambridge, MA: MIT Press.
Taylor, J. (2010). *Not a chimp: The hunt to find the genes that make us human*. Oxford, England: Oxford University Press.
Tomasello, M. (2014). *A natural history of human thinking*. Cambridge, MA: Harvard University Press.
Vygotsky, L. S. (1979). *Mind in society: The development of higher mental processes*. Cambridge, MA: Harvard University Press. (Original works published 1930, 1933, & 1935.)
Wagner, P. A. (1983). The nature of paradigmatic shifts and the goals of science education. *Science Education, 67*(5), 605–13.

Wagner, P. A. (1990). Will education contain fewer surprises for students in the future? In V.A. Howard (ed.), *Varieties of thinking* (pp. 142–75). New York, NY: Routledge.

Wagner, P. A. (2011). Socio-sexual education: A practical study in formal thinking and teachable moments. *Sex Education, 11*(2), 193–211.

Wagner, P. A. (2013). Game theory as psychological investigation. In H. Hannapi (ed.), *Game theory relaunched* (pp. 325–44). Rijeka, Croatia: Intech Open Access pub. http://dx.doi.org/10.5772/53932.

Wagner, P., Johnson, D., Fair, F., & Fasko, D. (2016). *Thinking beyond the test: Strategies for re-introducing higher-level thinking skills.* Lanham, MD: Rowman & Littlefield.

Wagner, P., & Lopez, G. (2010). The great conversation and the ethics of inclusion. *Multicultural Perspectives, 12*(3), 167–72.

Wagner, P., & Simpson, D. (2009). *Ethical decision making in school administration.* San Francisco, CA: Sage.

Wainer, H. (2016). *Truth or truthiness: Distinguishing fact from fiction by learning to think like a data scientist.* Cambridge, England: Cambridge University Press.

Warneken, F., & Tomasello, M. (2008). Extrinsic rewards undermine altruistic tendencies in 20-month-olds. *Journal of Developmental Psychology, 44,* 1785–88.

Weller, J. A., Levin, I. P., & Denburg, N. L. (2011). Trajectory of risky decision making for potential gains and losses from ages 5 to 85. *Journal of Behavioral Decision Making, 24*(4), 331–44.

Wiles, A. (1995). Modular elliptical curves and Fermat's last theorem. *Annals of Mathematics, Second Series, 141*(3), 443–551.

Wiley, R. (2015). *Noise matters.* Cambridge, MA: Harvard University Press.

Wittgenstein, L., & Anscombe, G. E. M., trans. (1953). *Philosophical investigations.* New York: MacMillan.

Worley, P. (2015). How to philosophize with children. *The Philosopher's Magazine, 69*(2), 98–104.

Zagzebski, L. (2012). *Epistemic authority: A theory of trust, authority and autonomy of belief.* Oxford, England: Oxford University Press.

# Author Index

Adams, Abigail, 51
Adams, John, 51
Aquinas, Thomas, 69
Ariely, D., xv
Aristotle, 2, 33, 45, 46, 50, 52, 53, 66, 86, 87
Augustine (saint), 67
Axelrod, R., 1

Bailin, Sharon, 74
Barrows, John, 26
Battersby, Mark, 74
Baudet, Stephanie, 72
Bazerman, M. H., xv
Becker, Gary, 2
Bentham, Jeremy, 65
Berwick, Robert C., 4
Bicchieri, Cristina, 2, 5
Bloom, Benjamin, 2, 3
Boole, George, 2
Bowles, S., 1, 4, 11
Brothers, Dr., 66
Brown, Dan, 48
Bruner, Jerome, 2
Burroughs, Michael D., 72

Camus, Albert, 66
Cantor, Georg, 80
Carter, Jimmy, 46
Castelli, I., 2
Chavez, C. A., 2

Chomsky, Noam, 4
Christian, B., 8
Cleghorn, Paul, 72
Confucius, 33
Curie, Marie, 40

Dali, Salvador, 15
Darwin, Charles, 1, 22
Dawkins, Richard, 22
Denburg, N. L., 3, 4
De Waal, Frans, 1
Dewey, John, 3, 80

Ebbesen, W. E., 4
Eccles, John, 64
Einstein, Albert, 22, 40
Epictetus, 67
Epicurus, 66
Euclid, 8

Facione, Peter, 74
Fair, F., 3
Fasko, D., 3, 74
Fehr, E., 2
Fermat, Pierre, 6, 7
Festinger, Leon, 79
Feynman, Richard, xiv
Fischbacher, U., 2

Gachter. S., 2
Gigerenzer, Gerd, 74

Gilovich, Tom, 74
Gintis, H., 1
Gittens, Carol, 74
Gneezy, U., 2, 10
Gopnik, A., 4, 5
Gould, Stephen Jay, 22
Grant, Amy, 7
Grant, R., 10
Griffiths, T., 8

Hacking, I., 9
Hamilton, W., 1
Hand, David, 56
Hanson, Norwood, xiii
Hawking, Stephen, 26, 40
Hemberger, Laura, 72
Hempel, Carl, 55, 56
Heraclitus, xiii
Herrmann, B., 2
Highfield, R., 5, 10
Hillis, Danny, 8
Hobbes, Thomas, 49
Horsten, L., 9
House, Bailey, 4, 5
Hume, David, 33
Huxley, Thomas, 68

James, William, 19–21
Jefferson, Thomas, 51–52
Johnson, Daphne, 3, 72

Kahneman, Daniel, 2, 74
Kennedy, John, 51
Khait, Valerie, 72
King Jr., Martin Luther, 51, 54
Koertge, N., 9
Kohlberg, Lawrence, 2
Kuhn, Deanna, 72
Kuhn, Thomas, xiii, xiii–xiv

Lacewing, M., 7
Laura, Dr., 67
Leighton, R., xiv
Levin, I. P., 3, 4
Lipman, Matthew, 3, 72, 73, 80
Lone, Jana Mohr, 72, 73
Lopez, G., 9
Lord, E., 7
Lynch, M. P., 77

Maguire, B., 7
Marchetti, A., 2
Massaro, D., 2
McClintock, Barbara, 40
Michelangelo, 17
Mill, John Stuart, 77
Miller, George, 2
Miller, Roger, xiii
Mischel, W., 4
Mlodinow, L., 1, 4
Moore, B. R., 1, 6
Moore, G. E., 69
Mother Teresa, 46

Nash, John, 2, 69
Necker, Louis Albert, 2
Newton, Isaac, 22
Nisbett, Richard, 74, 89
Nosich, Gerald, 73
Nowak, Martin, 1, 5, 10

Obama, Barack, 84
Olson, K. R., 4
Oscanyan, Frederick, 72
Oyler, Joe, 73

Paul, Richard, 3, 73
Perkins, David, 73
Phil, Dr., 66, 67
Piaget, J., 2, 13
Plato, 33, 63, 65, 69, 78
Polkinghorne, John, 26
Pollock, Jackson, 28, 44
Putnam, Hilary, 41

Raeburn, P., 3, 6
Rawls, John, 32
Reagan, Ronald, 51
Rodin, 17
Rousseau, Jacques, 49
Rustichini, A., 2, 10
Ryle, Gilbert, 35, 85, 86

Sartre, Jean-Paul, 66
Schlesinger, Dr., 66
Schroeder, Gerald, 26
Sharp, Ann Margaret, 72
Simon, Herbert, 2
Simpson, D., 10

Smith, Adam, 5
Sober, Elliot, 68
Socrates, 33, 78
Spelke, E. S., 4
Stanovich, Keith, 74
Sternberg, Robert, 3

Taleb, Nassim, 56
Tarski, Alfred, 36
Taylor, J., 1, 5
Tenbrunsel, A. E., xv
Thoni, C., 2
Tipler, Frank, 26
Tomasello, M., 1, 11

Vaughn, Lewis, 74
Vygotsky, L. S., 84

Wagner, Paul, xiii–xiv, 3, 4, 9, 10, 12
Wainer, H., 1, 9
Waller, Bruce, 74
Warneken, F., 11
Wartenberg, Thomas, 72
Weinberg, Steven, 26
Weller, J. A., 3–5
Wiles, Andrew, 6–8
Wiley, Robin, 6, 77
Wilson, David Sloan, 68
Winfrey, Oprah, 66
Wittgenstein, L., 81
Worley, P., 4, 12

Zagzebski, L., 87
Zeiss, A., 4
Zollman, K., 3, 6

# Subject Index

actions, 80
ad hominem, 98
Affirming the Antecedent, 90
Affirming the Consequent, 91, 92
altruism, 5, 6, 10, 11; reciprocal, 68
anecdotes, 94
appeal to authority fallacy, 97
appeal to common practice, 97
appeal to popularity, 97
appeal to traditional wisdom, 97
appropriate language, 82–84
*Argue with Me* (Kuhn, Hemberger, Khait), 72
argumentation mindware tools, 96–98
art, middle school script, 14–16
assumptions, 8
awesome, middle school script, 16–17

beauty: gifts that are beautiful, 46–47; middle school script, 17–18
begging the question, 97
beliefs, 35, 36; change in, 80
bias, 93–94
*Big Ideas for Little Kids* (Wartenberg), 72
*Black-Body Theory and the Quantum Discontinuity, 1894–1912* (Kuhn), xiv
black swans and induction, script, 55–56
bowing, 36, 37
"Brain in a Vat," secondary school script, 41–42

causation, 95
censorship, 54
chance: "chances are", 42–43; design and, 44–45
classical fallacies, 96–98
classical theory of governmental purpose, 49–53
cognitive, 83
cognitive psychology, 4
community of inquirers, 6–9; books on engaging students in, 72
compassion, 2
confirmation bias, 92
confounding, 96
Connection Machine, 8
consciousness, middle school script, 18–19
contradictions, 54–55
convenience sample, 96
correlation, 95
critical review, 7, 8
critical thinking, xv; philosophy and, 2; resources, 74–75
*Critical Thinking and Reasoning: Current Research, Theory, and Practice*, (Fasko), 74
*Critical Thinking: Consider the Verdict* (Waller), 74

*The Da Vinci Code* (Brown), 48
Declaration of Independence, 51

deductive reasoning, mindware tools: deductive validity as fundamental concept, 89–90; "if" connections, 90–92
deductive validity, 89–90
Denying the Consequent, 91
design: chance and, 44–45; secondary school script, 43–45
Dictator Game, 5
difference, middle school script, 19–21
DNA, 47–48
doubting, middle school script, 25–26
dreaming, 42
duties, rights and, 54, 62

Epicureans, 66, 67
evidence, suppressed, 97–98
evolution, 68; good life and, 64; middle school script, 22
existentialists, 66, 67
expressionists, 15

facts, 36
fairness, 32
fallacies, classical, 96–98
false dilemma, 97
Founding Fathers, governmental purposes and, 51–53
free speech, 10–11
friends: of common interest, 45; of common motivation, 45; authentic gifts and friendship, 45–47; of shared well-being, 46

generalizing, 93–94
genes, secondary school script, 47–48
gifts: beautiful, 46–47; of common purpose, 46; friendship and authentic, 45–47; ugly, 46
good life, secondary school script, 63–67
governmental purpose: Founding Fathers and, 51–53; secondary school scripts, 48–53
gravity, 22
Great Conversation, 3–6; community of inquirers and, 6–9; institutions for student involvement in, 72–74; as paradigm of social organization, 9–12; as social paradigm, 6–12

hand shaking, 36–37
happiness, governmental purpose and, 52
Harvard University, Project Zero, 73
"hide and seek" discussions, 81
*How We Know What Isn't So* (Gilovich), 74

IAPC. *See* Institute for the Advancement of Philosophy for Children
ideas: idea enzymes, 54–55; profound, important, and powerful, 34
"I dunno", middle school script, 22–25
"if" connections, 90–92
impressionists, 15
induction and black swans, script, 55–56
inductive reasoning, mindware tools: correlation and causation, 95; randomized comparative trial, 96; sampling and generalizing, 93–94
inferential mechanics, 9
*Informal Logic*, 75
*Inquiry: Critical Thinking Across the Disciplines*, 74–75
Institute for the Advancement of Philosophy for Children (IAPC), 73
intolerance, 54

kissing, secondary school script, 57–58
knowing: "Brain in a Vat" and, 41–42; knowing how, 85; knowing that, 85; man's way of, 39–41; woman's way of, 39–41

language: appropriate, 82–84; of mathematics, 6; thinking and, 1, 4, 6
law, middle school script, 27–28
*Leaning to Think Things Through: A Guide to Critical Thinking* (Nosich), 73
liberal theory of governmental purpose, 49–53
logical operators, 87–88
love: cancer and, 60; romance, Valentine's Day, and, 58–61

*Making Learning Whole: How Seven Principles of Teaching Can Transform Education* (Perkins), 73
mathematics, language of, 6
*The Matrix*, 41

man's way of knowing, 39–41
mermaid wishes, middle school script, 30–31
middle school scripts, xv; art, 14–16; awesome!, 16–17; beauty, 17–18; consciousness, 18–19; different, 19–21; doubting and "why?" question, 25–26; evolution, 22; I dunno, 22–25; law, 27–28; mermaid wishes, 30–31; morality, 36–37; painting, 28; profound, important, powerful ideas, 34; promising, 28–30; risk, 31–33; social science, 33; tips for successful usage, 13–14; truthing, 34–36
mindware: argumentation tools, classical fallacies, 96–98; deductive reasoning tools, 89–92; inductive reasoning tools, 93–96; overview, 89; toolkit, 98
*Mindware: Tools for Smart Thinking* (Nisbett), 74
Montclair State University, IAPC, 73
morality: middle school script, 36–37; secondary school script, 67–69
mutual respect, 10, 11

natural selection, 22
neuroscientists, 64
*Noise Matters* (Wiley), 77

obligations, 29

P4C. *See* Philosophy for Children
painting, middle school script, 28
paradigm shifts, xiii
paternalism, 62
*The Philosophical Child* (Lone), 72
philosophy, and thinking, 2–4
Philosophy for Children (P4C), 73
*Philosophy in Education* (Lone and Burroughs), 72
*Philosophy in the Classroom* (Lipman, Sharp, Oscanyan), 72
*The Power of Critical Thinking* (Vaughn), 74
primitivists, 15
Principle of Familiarity, 85–86
probably versus probability, script, 61–62
problems, framing, 5, 8
Project Zero, Harvard University, 73
promising, 1; middle school script, 28–30

questionable analogy, 98

randomized comparative trial, 96
reason, 80, 82; plausible, 80
reasoning: deductive, 89–92; inductive, 93–96; teaching, xiv–xv
*Reason in the Balance* (Bailin and Battersby), 74
reciprocal altruism, 68
representative sample, 94
respect, 37
rights, duties and, 54, 62
risk: middle school script, 31–33; secondary school script, 62–63
*Risk Savvy: How to Make Good Decisions* (Gigerenzer), 74
"Rock, Paper, Scissors", 61
romance, love, and Valentine's Day, script, 58–61

sameness, 20–21
Sam Houston State University (SHSU), 71–72, 74
sampling, 93–94
SAPERE, 73
satisficing, 5–6
science, 33
scripts, 3, 4; overview, 11–12. *See also* middle school scripts; secondary school scripts
scripts, building: appropriate language, 82–84; conclusion, 81–82; considerations, 82–87; critical review, 79–81; focus, 78; follow up, 79; kick off, 78–79; length, 84; overview, 77–78; picking topic, 78; relevant examples, 84–85; sneaking in names of scholars, 85–87; as your own, 87–88
scripts, writing, 71; SHSU website and, 71–72
secondary school scripts, xv; "Brain in a Vat", 41–42; chances are, 42–43; design, 43–45; Founding Fathers and governmental purposes, 48–53; friendship and authentic gifts, 45–47; genes, 47–48; good life, 63–67; governmental purposes, 48–53; idea

enzymes, 54–55; induction and black swans, 55–56; kissing, 57–58; love, romance, and Valentine's Day, 58–61; probably versus probability, 61–62; risk, 62–63; why be moral?, 67–69; woman's way of knowing, 39–41
self, and love, 59–60
self-interest, 5, 6
semantic clarity, 8
SHSU. *See* Sam Houston State University
slippery slope, 98
social norms, 5
social science, middle school script, 33
social studies, 33
STEM education, xiv, 3
stoicism, 67
Straw Man fallacy, 97
street dialogue, 8
*The Structure of Scientific Revolutions* (Kuhn), xiii
suppressed evidence, 97–98
surrealists, 15

theory, 22
*THINK Critically* (Facione and Gittens), 74
thinking: language and, 1, 4, 6; philosophy and, 2–4; potent thinking practices, 3–6; studies, 2–3; as symbol manipulation, 2. *See also* critical thinking
*Thinking, Fast and Slow* (Kahneman), 74
*Thinking and Reasoning*, 75
Thinking Machines Corporation, 8
*Thinking Skills and Creativity*, 75
*Thinking Through Philosophy* (Cleghorn and Baudet), 72
tolerance, 54
truth: truthing, 34–36; relativity of, xiii; search for, 9
two wrongs make a right (unthinking retaliation), 98

Ultimatum Game, 5
University of Hawaii, at Manoa Uehiro Academy for Philosophy and Education, 72
University of Washington, Center for Philosophy for Children, 73
unthinking retaliation (two wrongs make a right), 98

Valentine's Day, 45–47; love, romance, and, 58–60
validity, 89–90

Weighing Reasons Conference, Princeton, 7
"whatever" discussions, 81
*What Intelligence Tests Miss: The Psychology of Rational Thought* (Stanovich), 74
"why?" question, middle school script, 25–26
woman's way of knowing, secondary school script, 39–41
"You Must Have Been a Beautiful Baby", 17

# About the Authors

**Paul A. Wagner**, PhD, is the author of over 130 publications. He holds a joint appointment in both the College of Education and the College of Human Sciences and Humanities at the University of Houston–Clear Lake. He has held various professional affiliations with each of the University of Houston campuses, Harvard, Stanford, Yale, and the University of Missouri. At the college level, he has taught economics, management theory, organizational behavior, development of the sciences, and a variety of courses in philosophy, psychology, and education. He has served on the American Philosophical Association's Committee on Pre-college Philosophy; he was vice-president of the Association of Philosophers in Education and president of the Central Division; and he also served as the executive secretary of the Philosophy of Education Society and on the Ethics Committee of the 40,000-member American Association of Public Administrators. He served on the Steering Committee of the Host City Committee of the second NAFTA conference and on the Board of Directors of a number of charities and civic organizations including Leadership Houston. His most recent publications have dealt largely with decision theory.

**Daphne D. Johnson**, PhD, is a professor of education at Sam Houston State University where she received the College of Education Outstanding Teaching Award. She received her doctorate in educational psychology and individual differences at the University of Houston–University Park. She served as the department chair for the Department of Curriculum and Instruction for seven years, bringing project-based learning to the educator preparation program. She worked with Dr. Frank Fair and other team members to replicate a study from Scotland on the effects of philosophy for children at a middle school in Texas. For the results, see "Socrates in the schools from Scotland to

Texas: Replicating a study on the effects of a philosophy for children program" (2015) *Journal of Philosophy in Schools* 2(1), pp. 18–37, and "Socrates in the schools: Gains at three-year follow-up" (2015) *Journal of Philosophy in Schools* 2(2), pp. 5–16. She is on the editorial board of the journal *Inquiry: Critical Thinking Across the Disciplines*. Currently, to further develop critical thinking in students, she directs the website http://thinkingbeyondthetest.weebly.com

**Frank Fair,** PhD (University of Georgia), is a professor of philosophy at Sam Houston State University, where he received the University's Excellence in Teaching award. He served as the managing editor of the journal *Inquiry: Critical Thinking Across the Disciplines,* and co-authored (with Vic Sower) *Insightful Quality: Beyond Continuous Improvement.* In recent years, his research and writing have been on the theory, practice, and pedagogy of critical thinking, on the creation of communities of inquiry in public school classrooms, and on innovation in organizations. He and Daphne D. Johnson were members of a team that replicated, at a middle school in Texas, an important study from Scotland on the effects of a Philosophy for Children program.

**Daniel Fasko Jr.,** PhD (Florida State University), is professor of educational psychology at Bowling Green State University. He teaches undergraduate and graduate courses in educational psychology and life-span development, as well as an honors seminar on creativity. He has held leadership positions in the American Educational Research Association and the American Psychological Association, and is a fellow of the Psychonomic Society. He is a frequent presenter, discussant, reviewer, and chair of sessions at national and international conferences. His research interests include critical and creative thinking and moral reasoning. He is former editor of *Inquiry: Critical Thinking Across the Disciplines,* and is ad hoc reviewer for *Psychology of Aesthetics, Creativity, and the Arts* and *Informal Logic*. Dan co-edited (with Wayne Willis) *Contemporary Philosophical and Psychological Perspectives on Moral Development and Education* (2008) and edited *Critical Thinking and Reasoning: Current Theory, Research, and Practice* (2003). In 2000, Morehead State University honored him as Distinguished Researcher.

www.ingramcontent.com/pod-product-compliance
Lightning Source LLC
Chambersburg PA
CBHW032029230426
43671CB00005B/245